An individual joins a

himself

꙰꙰꙰꙰꙰꙰

T-Groups and
Therapy Groups
in a Changing Society

Dee G. Appley and Alvin E. Winder

Foreword by Vladimir A. Dupré

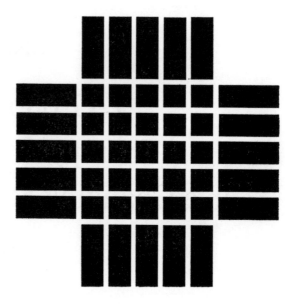

T-GROUPS
AND
THERAPY GROUPS
IN A
CHANGING
SOCIETY

Jossey-Bass Publishers
San Francisco • Washington • London • 1973

T-GROUPS AND THERAPY GROUPS IN A CHANGING SOCIETY
by Dee G. Appley and Alvin E. Winder

Copyright © 1973 by: Jossey-Bass, Inc., Publishers
615 Montgomery Street
San Francisco, California 94111
&
Jossey-Bass Limited
3 Henrietta Street
London WC2E 8LU

Library of Congress Catalogue Card Number LC 73-10934

International Standard Book Number ISBN 0-87589-201-9

Manufactured in the United States of America

JACKET DESIGN BY WILLI BAUM

FIRST EDITION

Code 7341

ぶぶぶ烏烏烏

The Jossey-Bass
Behavioral Science Series

Foreword

To be where it's at is to be in a group. Encounter. Sensitivity. T-group. Bio-energetics. Group therapy. Everywhere there are opportunities, not only available but thrust upon all of us. How can we choose? What's best for my particular need to change, explore, or experience? Who are the leaders and how competent are they? As a professional, interested in the practice of group therapy, sensitivity training, or personal growth awareness, what theory and method serves change and or growth needs?

An overwhelming variety of approaches faces the potential client. The prospective professional contemplates the tremendous diversity of practice with confusion.

In ten years the field of group practice has moved from a relatively monolithic, low profile situation to pluralism with a vengeance on center stage. The stage is full of ferment and change, shifting players in bizarre costume, and blurred images. A plethora of special language, devices, tricks, and forms obscure the underlying scene, preventing clear recognition of fundamental patterns of action and belief. The vigorous changing flow prevents enough sustained attention to discover basic themes.

The critical need in the field at this time is a sorting out process. This would permit penetration of the melee for a look at the core elements of group practice, for an ordering of the confusion. Such a professional look would reduce the confusion by identifying essential differences between the players, sharpening theoretical and practice issues, and encouraging research. The recent period of dynamic growth has contributed significantly to opening boundaries, destroying segmentation of disciplines, and adding new vitality to the earlier orthodoxy. These goals have been achieved and it is now time for the ordering process.

The authors of this have done just that, providing a significant contribution to clarifying the current chaos. Their overview of the scene divides group practice into two primary areas: T-groups and therapy groups. No intensive effort is made to examine the vast sub-areas within these categories. Rather, clarification is provided by "purifying" each, thus highlighting basic differences. This process helps the prospective professional, for whom the book is written, to understand the differences between T-group approaches and group therapy along the dimensions of underlying assumptions, goals and outcomes, values, approach to group dynamics, roles of members and the leader, education for practice, and research results.

The book is especially valuable to the student because it provides a guide, by doing the following: (1) Forcing a confrontation with central issues: For what purpose is a group formed? Who belongs? What is required of a leader in the group? What is the nature of the contract between the leader and group members? (2) Pointing to unresolved areas for further exploration. (3) Placing each orientation to group practice in the context of its intellectual origins with their different values and orientations. (4) Continuously explicating research findings and theory, and providing an excellent set of citations which lead the student to original sources. (5) Differentiating the group dimensions used in each field. (6) Providing a useful framework for conceptualizing the difference between group therapy and T-groups as the difference between "help-giving" and "help-sharing." Their concept may be fruitfully used in further research and analysis.

Challenges remain. As the book demonstrates so well, unresolved issues are numerous in both fields. Common to both are concerns about: The role of research; the integration of theory, research and practice; and the balance between being open to change and protecting standards.

The field of T-group training, as those of us actively engaged in its development are vividly aware, has special concerns, which center around: (1) Professionalization: the criteria for accreditation and the content of training. (2) Transfer of learning. (3) Translating laboratory change into on-going personal and, or, organization change. (4) Clearly differentiating among approaches in the personal growth (T-group) field.

In so clearly and accurately calling attention to these issues, the authors force us to take a long overdue, dispassionate professional look at what has been happening and what needs to be done in the future. This is especially relevant for the T-group, which in its more widespread applications has taken on aspects of being a social movement with overtones of religion and recreation. Because it is often seen as a symbol for man's search for new values, for overcoming the sense of alienation prevalent in modern society, practitioners need to be more conscious of the base from which they work and the implications of their practice for the larger social scene. If they assume the more extended role of social interveners in personal lives, work, and community, it is imperative that the added social responsibility be examined along with the professional issues. More than ever, value issues must be confronted.

As the authors propose, the T-group with its help-sharing approach offers an alternative model to the traditional help-giving practice of group psychotherapy. The implications of this view reach widely, reflecting or perhaps leading the way toward a new system of helping people to change and grow.

and that they would personally be involved in an on-going T-group which would meet once weekly for three hours during the semester.

Almost half way through the T-group experience, several students expressed the need and desire to deal with personal problems that were part of their outside-the-group day-to-day lives. To deal with these matters, the trainers believed a change would be required from a T-group format to a group therapy format. The trainers presented their thoughts to the group but agreed that they would be willing to change their roles from trainers to therapists if the group arrived at a consensual decision to do so. The trainers made it clear that they could not work on therapy problems in the trainer role. The group struggled with this problem and after two sessions arrived at a consensual decision to change to a therapy group.

Since the trainers/therapists were also the instructors, a major concern was how to highlight the differences and compare the similarities between the two group approaches. This particular chance development in the experiential part gave an unusual opportunity to make the distinctions very clear.

As a procedure for further highlighting the similarities and differences between the two experiences, which had been emerging with such clarity, the instructors hit upon the idea of successive terminations for both group experiences. The therapy group was terminated first, and the T-group was then reconstituted. The ending of the T-group followed two sessions later.

This experience provided us with the impetus to clarify first for ourselves, and then to share with others, the learnings that emerged from the experience. These learnings can be roughly divided into four categories: the group structure or climate, the role of the member, the role of the leader, and the group dynamics. The climate of the T-group enabled the development of shared leadership: students and trainers related to each other as collaborators and shared the responsibility for group maintenance before the changeover to the therapy group. The structure of the therapy group led to a regressive dependency of the members on the therapists: responsibility for the direction of the group and for group maintenance was readily relinquished to the therapists. It was dramatic to see the members who had been relating to each other in the T-group as adult peers relate in the therapy group as competitive, jealous, and possessive siblings. It was easy for the therapists to interpret these behaviors as related to transference reactions on the part of the members.

A marked contrast in the group dynamics of the two groups was the change-over from the free and open feedback of the T-group to the defensive and resistance-laden communication of the therapy group. In the training group, the trainers were able to be part of an interdependent network of relationships; "Al" and "Dee" dramatically became "Dr. Winder" and "Dr. Appley" in the transition to the therapy group. When the therapy group terminated, it was most apparent that both therapists represented parent figures and that the group members were working through some aspects of the conflict attendant upon emancipation from one's parents. The T-group parting witnessed the disappearance of Drs. Winder and Appley and the return of Al and Dee, and was marked by a warmth of expression among all members and a feeling on the part of the trainers that friendships were being renewed and confirmed and would be continued.

While many of these learnings have appeared in the literature of both fields and represent problems people have been struggling with for many years, the authors feel that their way of dealing with the issues at stake may be of some value to professionals and students who are seeking an introductory understanding to these two areas of group process. Although professional associations and journals have recently given a great deal of space to the issues raised by the burgeoning of human relations and group therapy practice, there still is a good deal of confusion and searching for clarification. The mass media—from major television networks to ever-popular women's magazines—have offered many explanations and illustrations of both kinds of group experiences, almost always mixing personal growth, encounter, T-groups, and therapy groups into something called "sensitivity" groups. In addition, there have sprung up a vast number of independent organizations and individuals offering a wide variety of group experiences to a receptive and responsive general public. Because of all these developments, it becomes especially important that there be some way of focusing on the critical differences between T-groups and group psychotherapy.

Preface

While *T-Groups and Therapy Groups in a Changing Society* has as its major aim the clarification of the distinction between the T-group and the psychotherapy group, it may be helpful at this point to offer a brief definition of each one. Group psychotherapy is a method for helping people with difficult personal problems, painful states of feeling, and emotional turmoil. A discussion group composed of fellow patients and a professional therapist is characteristic of this method. T-groups are training groups for people who want to learn something about themselves, group process, and decision-making in order to be effective members of groups and to share in leadership functions.

It is our intention to present group therapy and T-groups in parallel but polar positions; that is, to try to highlight their essential differences. We do not mean to say that there are "pure" therapy groups or "pure" training groups *as practiced* but that trainers and therapists have some responsibility for making their intentions (that is, style and philosophy) as clear as possible so that patients and other participants can seek out those experiences in which they are ready and willing to engage. As Bennis says, "I care far more about developing *choice* and recognition of choice points than I do about *change*. Change, I think, is the participant's privilege, but choice is something trainers must emphasize" (Bennis, 1969, p. 7).

As professionals, trainers and therapists do not have the luxury of using the group primarily for meeting their own needs, nor for making one-sided decisions for their clients. A trainer should not, even if qualified to do so, function as a "therapist" in a T-group unless the participants have agreed to be "patients" and have accepted this trainer as the therapist they wish to entrust themselves to. If an individual comes to a training group to deal with black-white relations and finds himself pressured to participate in a nude encounter, for example, and his refusal is "interpreted" for him as a psychological problem, this can be considered a tyranny imposed by authority and/or by false consensus of the group.

Similarly, an individual should not be accepted into a therapy group when he is really seeking a laboratory experience for his purposes; for example, he wishes to deal with here-and-now interpersonal phenomena, to find a collaborative help-sharing environment, and to be able to be more effective in a social action project such as improving prison conditions through the effective use of volunteers or creating a more optimal living-learning climate on a college campus.

We are not proselytizing either for therapy groups or for T-groups, nor suggesting the substitution of one monolithic system for another, for example, T-groups for therapy. We do, however, feel that the T-group has a broader function, with its purposes of individual growth and social change, while the therapy group is restricted to dealing with individuals who are in need primarily of personal change through a corrective emotional experience. As Strupp says, the therapeutic relationship "was seen as a way station to adult living in a complex world" (Strupp, 1973, p. 119).

T-Groups and Therapy Groups in a Changing Society is a plea for pluralism based on educated choices. Therefore, the emphasis is on *essential differences so that there can be real choices.* These are only two out of a number of possible choices. There are other kinds of group experiences including many variations of encounter groups which can serve the needs of people interested in personal growth experiences. We have chosen not to include the encounter group in this presentation. Although Gibb (1972) offers a generally positive presentation of what he terms "human relations training groups" (which includes the range of encounter groups), we feel strongly—along with Koch (1971) and Strupp (1973)— that the values inherent in encounter groups often run counter to the values basic to both group psychotherapy and the T-group. Both psychotherapy and T-groups are planned activities and place reason and intellect on a par with affect. However, many encounter groups offer instant need satisfaction and belittle the hard work and delayed gratification required of a participant in group psychotherapy. Nor is the encounter group directly related to the values the founders of the T-group held as reasons for developing a way of relating that would strengthen the democratic ethic and the scientific ethic in individuals and institutions. We believe also that the visibility of the encounter movement has served to obscure further the original purposes of therapy groups and T-groups. We see, therefore, the necessity of clarifying the distinctions between the two original forms as an important contribution to understanding therapy groups. However, such groups and methods have been very well described by others, from a professional and from a participant point of view, for example, Burton (1969), Howard (1970), Egan (1970), and Schutz (1967, 1971). These groups are usually offered as intensive, short-term experiences by a variety of help-giving individuals, some with a background in therapy. They offer expanded consciousness, increased awareness, and heightened emotional sensitivity.

These form part of a growing "human potential" movement, formal and informal, offering to help individuals develop more fully. The movement incorporates a whole range of activities including massage, meditation, and simulated rebirth; finger painting, dance, and simulated death; touching and being in touch. Every day "lots of people with no symptoms at all are dying" (Howard, 1971, p. xiii), and encounter and other personal growth groups attempt to help breathe life into such people as well as to relieve pain and to release joy. Many innovative ways will be created to meet the needs of human beings learning to live in the world as we move from a Darwinian, survival-oriented view of evolution to a Huxleyian (1961) or Teilhard de Chardinian (1959) vision of mankind's development.

Much less dramatic, but no less necessary in the meantime, are the reconstructive and re-educative experiences offered by group therapists and T-group trainers. We have written this book in the hope that these two important developments will henceforth be more clearly differentiated and better understood.

We would like to acknowledge our appreciation to the members of the group that served as the catalyst for our writing of this book, and to those individuals who have offered to share so freely their knowledge, encouragement, and time in support of our efforts. We wish to thank especially Ken Benne, Don Carew, Vlad Dupré, Martin Fischer, Max Rosenbaum, and Alice Sargent.

This book follows traditional English usage in accepting the pronoun *he* as adequate to refer to an individual, whether male or female. This decision reflects our sense of linguistic convenience, not our sexual politics.

Amherst, Massachusetts   DEE G. APPLEY
September 1973   ALVIN E. WINDER

Contents

ชชชชᏦᏦᏦᏦ

T-Groups and
Therapy Groups
in a Changing Society

theories challenged by the humanistic-experiential point of view, which is currently most widely represented by the encounter group movement.

The repressive-inspirational orientation is best represented by Pratt (1907, 1913), Lazell (1921), and Marsh (1931, 1935). Joseph Hersey Pratt, the first of this group to become interested in group psychotherapy, is considered by most writers in the field as the founder of American group psychotherapy. His first group consisted of a number of tuberculosis patients. His major concern as their physician was the care and management of their illness. Pratt, functioning as group leader, expressed himself as a physician in whom, as an authority on their illness, they could trust and believe. The work of Lazell followed, and his patient population, the hospitalized schizophrenic, was more properly in the psychiatric realm. Lazell, the psychiatrist-teacher, viewed group treatment primarily as a lecture series presented to patients. Marsh, a former minister who subsequently became a psychiatrist, worked extensively with groups of psychotic patients. His methods included religious revival techniques, formal lectures, and even art and dance classes.

Freud (1922), in 1909, brought his psychoanalytical concepts to America, shortly before the ideas expressed by psychoanalysis began to be accepted in the United States. Nevertheless, a quarter of a century elapsed before psychoanalytically oriented group treatment began to be practiced in this country. Four major contributors who have related psychoanalytic concepts of group treatment stand out during the period 1930 to World War II. They are Louis Wender (1936), Paul Schilder (1939), Trigant Burrow (1927) and Alexander Wolf (1949, 1950). With Wender's work, the psychoanalytic therapy group developed into the model used today. Groups consisted of six to eight members who were diagnosed psychoneurotic or borderline psychotic. Wender used the method of transference and selected partial personality reorganization as his goal. Schilder focused on the interaction between group members, and Burrow added the important but controversial point that the group, not the individual, was the necessary focus of successful psychiatric treatment. Finally, Wolf, working during and directly after World War II, integrated the theory and method of psychoanalysis into group psychotherapy. Following his lead, which greatly influenced the training of practitioners, psychoanalytical group therapists made use of the methods of transference, dream interpretation, historical re-creation, and free association.

Further major contributions to this area have been made by Fritz Redl (1966) and Samuel Slavson (1943). Both have worked extensively with children. Redl shows a marked talent in translating psychoanalytical concepts into the language of group process; his concepts of contagion and shock effect now are widely used in group psychoanalysis. Slavson, the originator of activity group therapy, developed a unique approach of modifying the group therapeutic experience to enable children to receive maximum treatment benefit from his procedure. He accomplished this by allowing activity to replace verbalization of conflicts, much as play therapy has been adapted to the treatment of children in individual analysis.

Shortly after World War II, the burgeoning of the group psychotherapy movement in America was paralleled with a sharp increase in interest in this field in Great Britian. Major developments were created by the group working at the Tavistock Clinic in London, particularly by Bion (1961) and Ezriel (1950, 1957). Bion found that he could characterize the emotional pattern of the group in terms of either a "W" (work group) or a "BA" (Basic Assumption) activity, which represented an antiwork group. The BA group was described further as BA Dependency, BA Pairing, or BA Fight-Flight. A given pattern might last for a few moments or several sessions. Bion experienced success in modifying these patterns through transference interpretations based upon interactions occuring in the phenomenology of the group. Ezriel observed that group action can be described in terms of three patterns of relationships. The first of these is the required relationship, and is established so that the group will not get involved in the second, which he called the avoided relationship due to group members' fear of the third, the calamitous relationship. Interpretations are focused upon the common group tension both for the group as a whole and for individual members.

A development of considerable interest to members of the group therapy profession on both sides of the Atlantic also emerged from the Tavistock Institute (Rioch, 1969). This development, called *group relations,* was, at its inception, heavily influenced by the contribution of group psychotherapy, especially the work of Bion, the social psychology of Kurt Lewin, and the work of the National Training Laboratories (NTL) in the United States (Trist and Sofer, 1959). Initially, emphasis was primarily on the study of small groups and secondarily on the problems encountered by group members in their work. Rice (1965) pioneered a major change in group relations when he directed the Tavistock conference toward providing an opportunity to learn about leadership. Rice and Miller (1967) wrote that the major task of members of a Tavistock conference group is to be aware of the group patterns that emerge when the group focuses on problems of leadership and authority. This task, they believe, is the "primary task" that an organization or institution must perform in order to survive. Emphasis is on the group as a whole, and when the group is "working" it is accomplishing its primary task.

Ackerman (1958), Bateson (1951), Satir (1964), and others have further modified the psychoanalytic model of the therapy group in the direction of family therapy, since they believe that the epitome of all conflict is within the family. Further, they believe this conflict can be resolved only within the family itself. The therapy group therefore is seen by them as an artificial group and an attempt to create a spurious family situation. For family therapists, the treatment group is the nuclear family and may include a range of three generations.

The humanistic-experiential orientation to group psychotherapy, although recent in development, has several major representatives, with the work of Eric Berne (1964), Fritz Perls (1969), and William C. Schutz (1967) best illustrating this orientation. Schutz represents the greatest break with the group therapy tradition. His theory of interpersonal needs holds that everyone needs inclusion, control, and affection, and that these needs can be expressed, fulfilled, or denied in one-to-one encounter and in group settings. Nonverbal communications including touching, embracing, and kissing are stressed and are used therapeutically to achieve self-awareness. Burton (1969) presents the rationale for the nonverbal approach with this statement: "The body has been strangely missing in psychotherapy and encounter attempts to return it to man."

The basic statement of Berne's transactional analysis involves an interaction between the patient and therapist in which the patient is required to understand the transactions occurring between his various ego states. Specifically, the goal of therapy is to put the adult ego state back into control so that the patient can be in a better position to make decisions about his life. Berne (1969) lists three steps as basic for building a strong adult ego: (1) learn to recognize your child, its vulnerabilities, its fears, its principle methods of expressing these feelings; (2) learn to recognize your parent, its admonitions, injunctions, fixed positions, and ways of expressing these; (3) be sensitive to the child in others, talk to that child, stroke that child, and appreciate its need for creative expression as well as the unfortunate burden it carries about. Transactional analysis like other experimental therapies focuses on experiences occurring in the here-and-now rather than on the historical reconstruction of patient motivations characteristic of psychoanalytical therapies.

Perls (1969) stresses that the Gestalt therapy is both humanistic and experiential. He states: "In Gestalt therapy we are here to promote the growth process and develop the human potential." Starting with the major premise of Gestalt Psychology that the whole is both greater and different from the sum of its parts, Perls stresses that the individual is a totality with constantly emerging needs. The therapist's position is to act as a catalyst to help these needs find self-expression so that the patient can express his real existence, as opposed to his phony role-playing. It is in the here-and-now that real existence occurs, concern with either the past or future represents pathology. Gestalt therapy groups differ from other experiential groups in that the therapist conducts individual therapy within the group setting. Perls calls these settings group seminars and group workshops.

The major controversy in group psychotherapy in the past decade, which promises to gain in intensity in the 1970s, is, in the words of Azima (1969, p. 259), "which way group therapists should vector themselves: deeper or broader, vertically or horizontally? There has developed a mystique or misconception that the deeper the core of personality penetrated, that is, the earlier the pregenital object relations brought into consciousness, the better the group process. The counter mystique is the proposition that the more the present phenomenological field interactions are discovered, the better. This latter emphasis has opened up the transactional, existential, and family approaches." The basic difference between the two approaches rests with the identification of the therapeutic method that leads to change.

For the adherents of the psychoanalytic model of group psychotherapy, the agent of change is the gradual development of insight in the individual. Such insight involves a conscious, clear, and satisfactory understanding of a pattern of behavior which is brought about through relevant transference interpretations by the therapist. Psychoanalytical-oriented group therapists differ in their approach to this problem. Some hold to the traditional psychoanalytical frame of reference that transference must be interpreted in terms of the transference neurosis resulting from a developmental conflict; others interpret the transference only in terms of the here-and-now relationship between the patient and the therapist. The latter group of therapists recognize the historical derivative nature of the transference but do not point out this aspect of the transference to the patient.

O'Hearne and Glad (1969, p. 269), speaking for the model of existential transactional group therapy, say the following about interpretation: "I believe that interaction in groups often makes it possible to bypass elicitation of insight in favor of enlarging ego boundaries and making it more likely that the patient will risk new action that may lead to increased present and future satisfaction. I believe that once the patient risks interaction, a reciprocal process, with one or more other persons, he learns that relationships with their feelings and activities are not as dangerous as he had feared. I believe that regressive transference neurosis is usually to be avoided in this type of treatment."

Perhaps the best way to give the reader a chance to gain a feeling for the difference between these two approaches to group treatment is to present a brief excerpt from each of two therapeutic sessions. The first reflects the successful use of insight and is taken from a pychoanalytically-oriented group in which Azima (1969, p. 263–264) was the therapist:

Mrs. N. S., an attractive, blond, spontaneous young woman of twenty-seven had no difficulty interacting in the group. She participated in most discussions, showing empathy, giving advice, and speaking very fully about her problem. For many weeks she talked about her four-year-old son who showed marked stranger anxiety, fear, and panic of staying in nursery school. Five other mothers and myself who made up the group listened and emoted with her. Shortly before Christmas, she reported that her son was making progress, and even though he put up a fuss each morning, she could leave him at the school. The following week she reported that the whole trouble was back. With prompting, she elaborated that, 'Jeff didn't look so good to me. I thought he was coming down with a cold, so I decided to keep him home Wednesday and Thursday.' One of the other members praised Mrs. S.'s preventive measure, and there was a discussion of the flu epidemic. I then commented on Mrs. S.'s anxiety and wondered if she could give more details. What gradually emerged was the fact that even though the boy really was not sick, she had kept the child home for the rest of the week, and the next Monday there was a return of the old panic and refusal to go to school.

The therapist pointed out that Mrs. S.'s behavior seemed to suggest both that she was not satisfied with the boy and that she had to prove to the child that her home was better than school. Deeper explanations were not given at this time. In later sessions it was learned that she had trained the boys (four and two) to go to bed at six in the evening. The group and I discussed her desire to have her husband to herself at night and to keep her sons close only to her. To deal with the situation she accepted the group's advice to give the boys a nap in the early afternoon, and in the following session she reported that the younger one had adapted well but that the problem child refused to nap or rest. Again, close listening revealed that what in fact was happening was that the mother had put the youngest in a bedroom but kept the four-year old with her in the living room, where she darkened the room, prepared a bowl of goodies, and watched TV. This time I pointed out with strong emphasis that again she had won her battle and reintensified the relationship between herself and the son. 'You make yourself and the setting so appealing that your son does not want to leave your side. You make him dependent on you for every gratification. At the same time you rule him and your husband.' Mrs. S. paled, bowed her head and said very quietly, 'I know I should have put him in the other room, but

I just forgot. It's funny you noticed when I sat on the sofa. What I want to say is I had two miscarriages before I could finally have Jeff, and then I watched him like a hawk. I never trusted anyone to look after him, until it was too late.' She then cried, 'How can he ever get out of my clutches!'

The following weeks showed a significant change in Mrs. S.'s attitude. She rescheduled her children, and the family began to have dinner together. The woman had been able to play-act the good mother and convince the group. Only via interpretation (but not to the point where she became aware that she was seducing her child and substituting him for her husband) was she able to change her behavior.

The following excerpt from a group session is presented to show from the transactional point of view how nonverbal behavior often can reveal both to the therapist and the group members deeper psychic functioning than words themselves are able to convey. O'Hearne (1969, p. 275–276) was the therapist.

An illustration which may show an advantage of interaction over verbalization occurred in a group in which I was treated warmly but deferentially by a young man who felt he should never succeed because his father had not. He had almost never expressed anger in his family or in the treatment group in an assertive way. He used much denial and intellectualization. He started one group session by saying, 'I sure was angry with you in my last individual session. You acted so sleepy and bored.' I replied, 'I was. I told you then that I was.' He answered, 'I know, but I couldn't feel my anger about it until later.' I said, 'You smiled all the way through.' He said, 'I couldn't feel angry then; I did later.' I asked, 'Are you angry now?' He answered, 'Of course.' I replied, 'I hear your words about anger, but I don't feel it.' He slumped his shoulders, smiled, sat with his legs wide apart, and assured me of his anger. I asked if he trusted himself with his anger and he said he did. I said, 'If you trust yourself with it, I will too. Let's try something. How about coming over here and placing your fist gently on my jaw?' The group laughed. As he doubled his fist, I said, 'Gently.' He placed his fist gently on my jaw and suddenly his smile left; he tried to get it back but couldn't. Tears formed in his eyes, and he pressed hard on my chin. He clenched his other fist, and I asked him if he wanted to put it on the other side of my chin. He very seriously said, 'No, I think I can control it, but I'm not sure.' He pulled it back a bit, kept it clenched, and I said, 'Can you feel anger now?' He backed away, nodded his head, and said, 'Now I know what it feels like. That's real anger.' The whole group was impressed with our trust. In the next two weeks, he stopped telling us how much he had changed and was improving; instead, he did something about his hostile-dependent relationships at home.

Table 1 presents a cognitive approach to the differences between the two therapeutic approaches.

Developments in practice within the 1960s can be listed under three major headings. These are: a concern for the furthering of conceptualization of the group processes, the exploration of practice with special populations, and a concern with the proliferation of group practices. The concern with conceptualization reached its high point in 1964 with the publication of four important books on group psychotherapy. Slavson, having finished his seven major papers on group process in the preceding year, published *A Textbook in Analytic Group Psychotherapy* in an effort to delineate his major theoretical contributions to the field. Berne's *Games People Play* is a popular version of his system of transactional analysis in which he describes the variety of games which people play in relationship to each other. Foulkes' *Therapeutic Group Analysis* updated and reassessed his contribution to group analysis. Whitaker and Lieberman in *Psychotherapy Through Group Process* discuss their use of group process as a mode of psychotherapy. The year 1964 also was a high watermark in the number of papers, seven, that concerned psychoanalytic theory and group therapy. Included were technical papers on transference, resistance, counter-transference, and the use of dreams in group therapy.

If one were to categorize the major concern of group therapists during the 1960s, it would be with practice, particularly with special populations which can be divided roughly into nonpsychotic adults, psychotic adults, and children. Practice with nonpsychotic adults continue to deal with groups of adult neurotics, the tradi-

Table 1. Similarities and Differences Between Psychoanalytic and Existential Transactional Group Psychotherapy

Therapeutic Process	Psychoanalytic	Transactional
Therapeutic agent of change	Patient undergoes gradual development of insight.	There is a reciprocal interaction between members and therapists.
Understanding	Patient develops a conscious understanding of behavior, involving cognitive learning; affect provides the climate for understanding.	Understanding often occurs through nonverbal experience. The experiencing of understanding is affective and action-oriented.
Therapist's Role		
Skills	Therapist analyzes transferences and resistances. Patients chose their own system of values.	Therapist acts as a model or catalyst; his purpose is to express emotions, teach values, and employ techniques of touching and action.
Affect	Therapist needs awareness of his own feelings in order to keep them out of the	Therapist uses his feelings about group members to provide the feedback necessary

	therapeutic process unless they can aid in understanding of patient's motivation. His focus is on the feelings and motivations of group members.	to bring about behavioral change.
Therapeutic Focus	Therapist's interpretation uses relevant historical material to separate past from current influences on behavior. Both there-and-then and here-and-now interpretations are used.	The therapist's interpretations of the members' behavior refer strictly to the here-and-now.
Therapeutic Goals	The goal of treatment is basic personality change involving the resolution of developmental conflicts. If this change is successful, the patient will learn on his own to take responsibility for his behaviors and actions.	The goal is patient behavior change, which is defined as the patient's willingness to take risks in the immediate situation. These risks are characterized by responsive behavior.
Process by which the group member is affected	Patient learns only when resistances to change (defenses) have been removed; he can learn from a positive group experience only when these resistances have been analyzed.	Patient learns through positive group experience and feedback.

tional concern of therapists in private practice. During the past decade such concern was widened to include both institutional and medical center populations. Institutional populations include alcoholics, prisoners, sex offenders, drug addicts, mentally retarded adults, and similar problem groups. Medical center populations include patients with a variety of psychosomatic conditions; for example, patients referred to group treatment include those suffering from post-cardiac conditions, bronchial asthma or multiple sclerosis. Rehabilitation is the goal of group therapy with both institutional and medical populations.

The disadvantaged and the college student are two populations that caught the interest of group therapists in the latter half of the 1960s. The War on Poverty initiated by the Kennedy and Johnson administrations dramatically brought the poor to the attention of psychotherapists, who, as a result, showed an increasing interest in the rehabilitation of people living under extremely disadvantaged conditions. This economically deprived group does not seem to understand the need either for insight into or the development of coping patterns to deal with their intrapsychic problems. Group therapists, in an effort to reach these individuals, have departed from their traditional roles as therapeutic group leaders to the roles of consultants to agencies working with the poor. Their consultations involve helping agency staffs locate and deal with stresses in the lives of their clients and locate and deal with dislocations in the social systems with which the clients have to cope or live.

The burgeoning numbers of unhappy and dissatisfied students on rapidly expanding college campuses have also received attention from many group therapists. Counseling groups have been introduced on campuses where students suffer from separation anxiety, loneliness, and depression. Other students have been confused by the complexity of the new university-cities that now characterize many colleges and universities. Still others have trouble in dealing with rapidly changing systems of morality that appear to be at great variance with their own upbringing.

Practice with psychotic adults centers around two groups. The predominant work has been done with groups of hospitalized schizophrenics. Groups presently are held not only with the patients themselves but also with their parents, their families, ward personnel, nurses, and residents in an effort to help the patient indirectly by working with those who are in closest interaction with him. The second group has been the hospitalized brain-injured. (Unfortunately, the pressing stress of social problems seems to have left group therapists little time to give to this population.)

Much recent group therapy and family therapy deals with children and adolescents, their parents, and families. Most notable is the impetus the 1960s gave to family therapy. In many agencies, family therapy tends to replace individual psychotherapy with emotionally disturbed children, supplemented by casework interviews with their parents. Children in need of rehabilitation also have profited from membership in psychotherapy groups. Some of these include the mentally retarded, the cerebral palsied, foster children, children with speech and learning problems, underachieving adolescents, and pregnant adolescents.

Concern with the proliferation of group practices and their relationship to the traditional models of group therapy reached its peak in 1968, a year designated by the *New York Times* as "the year of the group." A proliferation of marathons, minithons, encounter groups, sensory awareness groups, and growth groups deluged the general public and produced concerned articles in major journals in the mental health field. Some articles were highly critical and some were sympathetic. Major issues raised by those critical of the new movement were: first, the cultish quality of the new groups and their lack of specifically defined purpose or goals; second, the failure of group leaders to take responsibility for safeguarding the participants in these innovative group experiences; and, third, the lack of adequate definition of the necessary skills and training that should be possessed by the group leaders. Those who were sympathetic spoke of an increasingly permissive society with changing family ties and of a changing sense of values with the emergence of both new intrapsychic problems and new interpersonal modes of behavior. May (1969), in a terse but accurate statement of this change, refers to the 1950s as the decade of "anxiety," and the 1960s as the decade of the "identity crisis," and he views the 1970s as the period of the "crisis of will." Enthusiastic writers speak of such new group therapies as being developed for a new type of individual. Those who are sympathetic, but conservative, support the point of view that innovations in group therapy are healthy, but they ask that practitioners proceed with caution.

Research in group psychotherapy during the 1960s suggests that most practitioners remained relatively unconcerned about evaluation of their work. A survey conducted in the early 1960's reveals a "yes, research is important, but . . . " attitude on the part of many group psychotherapists. There was, in spite of this attitude, some developing momentum toward research in the latter half of the decade. The literature reviewer of the *International Journal of Group Psychotherapy* in 1964 felt that there were enough papers on research to include, for the first time, a special section headed "research" in his annual review of group therapy literature for that year. The effectiveness of a method of treatment, comparison between two types of treatment, and studies of specific aspects of group process such as decision-making and the relationship of be-havior to group satisfaction were characteristic of the studies re-ported in this period. Research publications in the field generally fall into three major categories. These are, first, those dealing with prediction of behavior during group treatment; second, studies dealing with the outcome of patient response to treatment; and third, studies of the group process itself. Examples of the first category include a prediction of group dropouts from the group interaction in the first meeting, a prediction of the subsequent relationships between group members based upon initial patient interactions, and a prediction of compatibility of group members based upon their scores on the Fundamental Interpersonal Relations Orientation Scale-B (a measuring instrument based upon the theory that every person orients himself toward others in characteristic ways which determine interpersonal behavior)'.

Among outcome studies, two major criteria have been used to measure changes resulting from treatment. These involve the use of intrapsychic criteria such as change in self-concept and behavioral criteria. Behavioral criteria include such easily observable indices of behavior as ability to hold a job, length of stay out of a mental institution, and change in grade point average. Studies of group process deal with various aspects of group functioning. The identification of critical incidents in the ongoing group, the development of group norms, the processes by which group consensus occurs, and an investigation of the decision-making process occurring within the group are examples of these kinds of studies.

MacLennon and Levy (1968, p. 316), in their review of the group therapy literature for 1967, sum up the then present status of research in this field: "Although there are many more reports of research in group treatment than in the past, there still remains a lack of coherence between goals, method and outcome, and a general uncertainty as to how to judge the quality of treatment and the effectiveness of therapists."

After a discussion of the major controversy in theory and some delineation of the current directions of practice and research, the next question is, what should the competent group therapist be? This question raises a number of issues for group therapist educators. Furthermore, these issues seem independent of whether the fledgling group psychotherapist has arrived at the threshold of a training program by way of medicine, psychology, social work, education, or the ministry.

A statement on issues in education requires restating a basic assumption that runs through the treatment of group psychotherapy in this book: namely, group therapy provides a different dimension of experience than does individual therapy, a dimension which is due to the social system provided by the multiple relationships inherent in the small group. Therefore, the group therapist must understand not only the nature of group interactions but also must be able to work with these interactions to bring about therapeutic changes within the group members. With this assumption in mind, one can turn to the issues in education involved in developing a model for the competent group psychotherapist. We are indebted in a discussion of these issues to Lakin, Lieberman and Whitaker (1969).

The question that the beginning student must ask himself is, what is the concept of help-giving to which I feel committed? This concept will differ with the professional and personal experiences of the student. Unfortunately, students coming out of many professional backgrounds (notably psychiatry, clinical psychology, nursing, and theology) may already have accepted the one-to-one relationship as the basic or only model of help-giving. Should this be the case, they must learn to live with the dyadic model yet learn to accept another new model, that of the group.

A second issue in education refers to the student therapist's understanding of both the group as a psychotherapeutic medium and of his role as a therapist working within it. The first understanding involves knowing the therapeutic dimensions of group interaction; for example, the group's ability to consensually define reality, to establish standards of behavior for members, to accept or reject the group roles members select for themselves, and the group's capacity to offer warmth and support to individual participants. The second understanding which is required of the student refers to his ability to know what is going on in the group and to his possession of the necessary skills of intervention and timing that permit him to intervene therapeutically in any group interaction.

The beginning therapist should have empathy for the patient. The collective powers of the group to isolate, to scapegoat, to support, and to demand conformity are largely unrecognized by those who are used to one-to-one relationships. The majority of group therapy educators strongly believe one must live through this dimension of group experience to appreciate its impact on group members.

A final issue concerns the understanding of the relationship of the group therapeutic role to the therapist's needs in the group. It long has been recognized by individual therapists that they can easily fall into the error of selecting a therapeutic role that meets their own needs for security rather than the patients' needs for therapy. This same issue applies to the group therapist who may select a therapeutic stance which he finds comfortable and rewarding. He may be most comfortable if he is powerful, distant, secretive, or authoritarian. While such postures may be unconsciously rewarding for the therapist, they may be unacceptable in their prevention of personal growth in the members. The adage "know thyself" that applies to therapists who work with individuals only applies equally well to those who would engage in group therapy.

After defining the model of the competent group psychotherapist, the next step is to outline the educational procedures designed to provide the experiences whose objective is to achieve this model. Most educational programs are characterized by a series of several steps. The first is generally a formal teaching experience in which the student hears lectures and does assigned reading. Concurrently with this formal experience, the student may be placed in a group composed of other students, one in which he is required to participate as a member. A third step involves the exposure of the student to groups through vicarious methods—a one-way screen, video tape, and so forth. A fourth step that may be used in conjunction with the previous one involves the therapist in training in role-playing exercises. Then the student is ready for the fifth step: He is allowed either to participate directly as group therapist or as cotherapist with a trained group leader. This final step may extend over a year or longer and is characterized by a close supervisory relationship between the student and a training therapist.

The recruitment and selection of appropriate candidates for training programs, the differing emphases these programs give to the role of the group therapist, and both the educational procedures and the designs of various programs all will be reviewed later in depth.

Chapter II

⋟⋟⋟⋞⋞⋞

Training Groups: History and Current Issues

In 1946, through a series of fortuitous circumstances and a generous amount of planning, a small group of men (whose individual commitment to the values of science and the values of democracy were strengthened by their work and each other over a period of years) began to collaborate as the staff for a workshop on intergroup relations in New Britain, Connecticut.

That workshop was to find itself immortalized as the ancestor of the training group (later T-group) and the human relations laboratory, and it became itself a model for an action research laboratory, defined as Kurt Lewin's model for studying a social problem by changing the situation and then systematically studying the effects (Lewin 1946, Sanford 1970), which might well still be emulated. An enterprise which involved interdisciplinary collaboration, it was congruent with what later were articulated as the metagoals and values of this model of training. The workshop was quite clearly a reeducation and social action project. Since then, this training method has been taken over by hundreds of "trainers" of varying degrees of competence, and hundreds of thousands of people have been participants; but the theory and the research which should be an integral part of the workshop method have been ignored; and even *action* has been redefined by whatever is done rather than what might be planned intentionally. It is certainly time to reexamine the value base out of which this method was born, since even some of its own adherents have recently expressed their concern about its validity or viability; its practitioners often are ignorant of its existence; and the very organization which has come to stand symbolically for this orientation, the National Training Laboratories, has recently been in the throes of needed major reorganization, at least in part because of questions about the mission of NTL.

Therefore, it seems very timely to trace the history of these reeducational innovations from modest beginnings in 1946 to the present seemingly endlessly expanding enterprises. What is a T-group? What is a human relations laboratory? Has another profession developed which can control its practitioners while its applied behavioral science twin encourages its theory builders and supports its researchers, while together science and practice accumulate and refine a shared body of knowledge, and where all act as planned change interventionists around a common set of values?

In the summer of 1946, some participants in the workshop were present as audience when the staff of the workshop met to discuss the behavior of the same participants as observed earlier in the day. The data had been gathered systematically on observation schedules by the research staff. However, discrepancies as well as confirmations of perceptions of the members' behavior and the group's interactions soon were shared by both audience and staff. And it was quickly recognized that *feedback*—the opportunity to give and receive personal perceptions of commonly shared data about each other's behavior and interactions—was a very exciting and powerful method for learning, and that the impact of this exchange was very great. If changing attitudes and behaviors were an important goal at the workshop, here indeed was an important procedure. The workshop henceforth was qualitatively changed with the acceptance of that accidental innovation, feedback.

The next summer (1947), such experience-based learning (which with some important modifications would be called a T-group in 1949) was deliberately designed into a summer session course offered for the first time at Gould Academy in Bethel, Maine —a place which since has become synonymous for many with the whole small group movement. This new method—a "back-home" problem-centered workshop for community leaders, with feedback sessions about here-and-now behavior, would come to be called a laboratory where participants could purposely examine their own behavior and group processes and try out social action solutions for problems they faced in organizations and institutions in their own communities. The more usual role-playing, case studies, and lectures would continue as complementary parts of the workshop.

In the 1946 workshop at New Britain, Connecticut, the thirty participants were mostly social workers and teachers, with some businessmen. All were concerned with the problems of inter-group relations. The professional staff included Kurt Lewin, a social psychologist whose interest in and commitment to action research had led to the enterprise, and whose theoretical formulations have had lasting influence on the field of group dynamics. Working with him as group leaders were three men who still actively contribute to the applied behavioral science and the emerging profession centered around laboratory training. These were Ronald Lippitt, a social psychologist who came with an interest in innovation in edu-cational processes, the effects of leadership style on group effective-ness, and action research as an approach to social change; Kenneth D. Benne, a philosopher interested in practical judgment, whose "studies led to the belief that there were principles and methods in democracy which, while consistent with principles of scientific method, in some ways went beyond them" and who had developed a "great awareness of the importance of a re-educative social process to work through differences within groups and among people in normative orientation, in goals, and in means" (Bradford, 1967, pp. 129–130); and Leland P. Bradford, who "was always concerned with building bridges to action, with developing educational innovation, and with finding better ways for people to discuss and solve problems" (Bradford, 1967, p. 130), and who brought a background of working with adult education projects in exciting new ways. All brought workshop experiences and a commitment to participation-based learning through problem-solving. A small staff of research assistants was another integral element in that historically important workshop.

Bradford (1967) recalls in a moving anecdotal style the circumstances under which, over a period of years it came about that he, Lippitt, Benne, and Lewin worked together during the summer that these two innovations in educational technology began to take form. Thus what might seem a happenstance event turns out to be part of a long-developing set of personal and professional relationships with common commitment to a set of values. Marrow (1967, 1969) adds his remembrance of Kurt Lewin, "the practical theorist," whose ideas and commitment to the work he was engaged in seemed to be the catalyst on many occasions which allowed possibilities to become realities.

The laboratory movement, that is, deliberately supervised, small-group human relations workshops such as those offered at Bethel by the organization later called the National Training Laboratories, developed out of the grave concern of educators and behavioral scientists who were interested in solving what they recognized as increasingly critical social problems, particularly in the area of human relations: problems caused by rapid technological growth, increased bureaucratization, and increased depersonalization. The development of social psychology early in the twentieth century, as well as such developments as the philosophy of progressive education along with the impact of psychoanalytic theory, contributed to the development of a climate for "the reformation and salvation of society not just the individual" (Gottschalk and Pattison, 1969).

Over and over again, however, it will be apparent that one important difference between human relations and other reeducative alternatives is a commitment to the idea of what "might be"—a commitment to a set of values coupled with a spirit of inquiry tied to a scientific body of knowledge. It is accompanied by the personal understanding by the scientist-practitioner that what is very much needed in society today is continuous planned change for organizational and institutional effectiveness plus the opportunity for individuals to have and maintain their integrity and exercise their influence. As Lewin once said, when reminded he was overworking and not well, "When you have to go to sleep each night, hearing the anguished screams of your mother as the brutal Nazis tortured her to death in a concentration camp, you can't think of taking it easy" (Marrow, 1967, p. 146). Social change was seen as an urgent necessity and training change agents as an urgent need.

All of these men had worked very hard to bring about the Connecticut workshop, but particularly Lewin, who finally was able to convince a financial sponsor to underwrite the remaining expenses. All of the staff were gratified with the results of the workshop, even Lewin. Tragically, he did not live to join the others at the first NTL session held in 1947. And, ironically, as Marrow tells us, "despite its successful outcome, neither of the two sponsors—the American Jewish Congress and the Connecticut Interracial Commission—has, in the subsequent years, continued its interest or sent members of its staff to NTL. The financial sponsor, after the workshop had ended, abruptly announced that he would no longer support any group dynamics research, and all but forty thousand dollars of his million-dollar grant was returned to him" (Marrow, 1967, p. 150).

Now began a period of development, of expansion and experimentation, which would force the prophets, proponents, practitioners, and participants to deal with all of the problems among themselves which they intended to help others solve; and the very technologies, the T-group and the laboratory, which were to be the instruments of such changes, would nearly be lost in the process by stretching almost beyond recognizable shape to cover more and more versions of themselves.

It would take all of the knowledge, skills, experience, and commitment of these scientist-philosopher-educators to preserve the viability of their vision of a scientifically-based, educationally-oriented and action-directed movement. And 1971 became a time for major reassessments; for making important decisions about persons accredited as trainers and those trained as participants; for determining the parameters of the T-group and the laboratory; for determining how these technologies shall be used as social system interventions and how the profession shall keep one foot firmly fixed in science and the other in practice; and how to select social action projects to pursue. "Cultures are maintained through the operation of self-validating processes. Changing a culture requires interventions that invalidate old processes and conditions that facilitate the creation of new self-validating processes" (Shepard, 1970, p. 259). In 1946, these two educational technologies, the training group and the training laboratory, began to assume identifiable sets of characteristics. Potentially these were, and are, examples of the kind of interventions that can help to invalidate old processes and provide conditions encouraging the creation and strengthening of new self-validating processes.

For a relatively short period of time, a group of people come together to learn consciously through their own experiences together how to make planned changes in old systems—whether that system be the individual, a small group or some larger unit of people—and to evaluate the effectiveness of their attempts. This is the laboratory approach to human relations training, and one important part of that laboratory is the T-group, a small artificially constructed primary group. Such activities can lead to extraordinary consequences if they are understood and can be implemented. The technologies could be invented in one workshop; to be understood could take the next twenty-five years.

In 1947, again under joint sponsorship of several institutions and staff from several disciplines, a three-week session was offered which included the Basic Skills Training Group. This was now seen as a place for learning *change agent* skills and concepts, and as a place for learning to understand and to help with group growth and development. This time there were thirty-seven staff and sixty-seven participants, and seven ambitious learning objectives were formulated: "(1) Help members internalize some more or less systematic concepts (including a schema for planned change and indices of group development). (2) Provide practice in diagnostic action skills of the change agent and of the group member and leader (including skill practice through role playing). (3)

Understand behavioral content as related to interpersonal and inter-group dynamics in organizations and less formal groups. (4) Plan the application of laboratory learnings to back-home situations, and plan for continuing growth for self and associates. (5) Gain more accurate view of self in relation with others and the group as a whole. (6) Develop a clearer understanding of democratic values (to operationalize these, an evaluation device was invented to measure changes in this dimension of learning). (7) It was also hoped the participants would acquire trainer skills" (Benne, 1964a, pp. 85–87). (As will be seen, the fifth objective became dispropor-tionately important, and by 1948, it became apparent that a three-week laboratory was not qualification enough for a trainer.)

Thus the training group as it developed at Bethel in 1947 was a three-week (later a two-week) residential community in which people could set learning goals for themselves, experiment with their own behavior in groups, and plan for effecting changes in the organizations and institutions with which they were regularly associated.

For the first two years, money was available from the Carne-gie Corporation only one year at a time, for the workshop was looked on as a temporary summer experiment. Nevertheless, the staff collaborated year-round through meetings and memoranda. They worked on papers which described the phases of planned change and what skills a change agent would need for each phase, on operational definitions for the phases of group development, a statement of democratic ideology as a guide for developing change agent skills, and the setting up of a comprehensive research pro-gram.

Staff observers still were responsible for feedback. Role-playing was practiced at interest groups and methods clinics; large town meetings were used for theory sessions and working out laboratory problems. Participants cooperated in research volun-tarily. In 1948, only minor changes occurred.

In response to a question from the Carnegie Corporation about the feasibility of others doing the training as well as the original staff, the stage was set for years of trying to resolve conflicts in methods, objectives, and theories by the inclusion of staff with other kinds of experiences and intentions. Most new staff who were invited in 1949 came from clinical and psychiatric backgrounds. Nor had they shared in the thinking of the first years when objectives were hammered out. Working within the democratic decision-making process, that very summer Benne, Lippitt, and Bradford were displaced as trainers and were given other tasks. (Coincidentally, at the end of that summer, Carnegie Corporation made it possible for NTL to become a year-round office, located within the National Education Association, and Bradford went to Washington to set it up. He became its first and only director until 1970, when Vladimir A. Dupré became director, and in 1971, president, of the reorganized NTL Institute for Applied Behavioral Science.)

During summer of 1949 there were many problems which, however, were not resolved. And the summer of 1950 was even more difficult. "T"-groups began to concentrate on intrapersonal and interpersonal learnings and became completely separated from "A"-groups, which were considered action groups and were to concentrate on skill training and social change. The most experienced laboratory staff became the T-group trainers; a separate staff became A-group trainers. By now, objective number five obviously was more and more separated from the others. Participants did not seem to find A-groups as interesting as T-groups, and there were intrastaff problems as well.

And so, what Benne calls Phase I of the T-group development, continued from 1949–1955. The T-group became increasingly separated from other parts of the laboratory. It had been apparent in 1948 that the list of learning objectives was very long and that some redefining of those objectives was necessary. At that time the participants still were thinking in the framework of stranger groups—that is, individuals who did not know each other but who came to a summer workshop for a one-time learning experience.

Each learning objective now began to have a separate grouping—role-playing, case studies, and so forth. The continuation of that trend led eventually to separate specialized laboratories: conflict resolution, consultation skills, and so forth. Obviously, trainers could not be turned out after one summer session, so that objective was eliminated after the 1948 session, although it set an expectation that is still held by many participants in such groups.

But given the limited time, how could all the other learning objectives be met? There were great differences of opinion, and many tensions developed, both within the clinical group (for example, Freudian versus Rogerian points of view) as well as between clinical and action-research-oriented staff. And the attraction for T-group experience (that is, learning about self and self in relation to others) remained strong on the part of participants as well as clinical staff.

Then began Phase II, which has continued since 1955: attempts to reintegrate the T-group into the laboratory. The question of transfer of learnings outside of the laboratory seemed very unlikely if the learnings could not be transferred inside the laboratory. Thus training for back-home application also suffered. To meet this problem, first occupational interest groups were set up, across T-groups, as a basis for back-home planning; then consultation units, with resource people to consult about back-home concerns of participants, were tried. Neither group was very effective —presumably they could not build enough trust in the short time available to utilize the opportunities for dealing with transfer. For several years this transfer to back-home was neglected, until it became obvious that the T-groups were the unit to use since they had already developed the trust level required.

Conceptual material—cognitive and ideological—also tended to disappear in those groups. More and more time and commitment to the experiential base developed. But there was not a very clear picture about what actually was going on in the T-groups since few records were kept and there was little sharing of experience. However, two facts did emerge as universally important: one was the central place of feedback; the other was the importance of the trainer for determining which objectives would be worked on and for creating the learning environment.

Obviously, the reintegration of the T-group with the other learning objectives had to be made since integrating learnings was the heart of this experience-based method. According to Benne, this reintegration has been attempted in three ways: "(1) The T-group centered laboratory: here the focus is on intrapersonal and interpersonal problems. The learning objectives are limited to those that facilitate these kinds of learnings, for example, skill practice in listening, and so forth. (2) The T-group is used for back-home transfer: all of the early learning objectives have been reintegrated. So there is focus on here-and-now learnings but participants also give and receive help on back-home problems. Use is made of competition and collaboration exercises, and change agent skills are practiced. (3) Different groupings are used with different technologies for different learning objectives. Integration is attempted by working on how to use laboratory learnings for back-home problems" (Benne, 1964a, adapted from pp. 107–109).

Further reintegration and resolution of tensions also were accomplished through other developments and innovations over the years: (1) through new training designs, (2) through conflict resolution among the staff, (3) through occupationally homogeneous laboratories (as opposed to the early heterogeneous basic laboratories), (4) through the development of regional laboratories —which set their own (limited) learning objectives—and (5) through alumni programs: different learning objectives could now be met over time (Benne, 1964a, adapted from pp. 109–111). Obviously, such reintegration is not complete, and, indeed, T-groups and laboratories now are defined by whatever it is that is being done in a group called a T-group or a "lab." A more definitive resolution through agreements around objectives, and verification of outcome effects through evaluation, is needed.

Bradford saw in these later developments three trends: "(1) Regional laboratories emerged autonomously—some of which have merged with or collaborated closely with NTL. (2) Occupational laboratories began to be held during the year instead of just in the summer, mostly in industry and religion. (3) NTL and network members have increasingly come to be engaged in organizational growth and development projects" (Bradford, 1967, pp. 142–143).

In the 1960s, recognition of these trends led to the reorganization of NTL into five centers: (1) Center for Organizational Studies, (2) Center for the Development of Educational Leadership, (3) Center for Community Affairs, (4) Center for the Development of Leadership in Government, and (5) Center for International Training. Later, in 1970, they became: (1) Center for Organizational Studies, (2) Center for the Development of

Educational Leadership, (3) Center for Black Studies, and (4) Center for a Voluntary Society. All became part of the renamed NTL Institute for Applied Behavioral Science.

However, in 1973, after the reorganization of the NTL Institute, these centers evolved into (1) Center for System Development, (2) Center for Macro-System Change, (3) Center for the Development of Individual Potential, and (4) Center for Professional Development.

At that time Bradford enumerated some hopes and concerns about the future of the Institute. He saw as "good developments" the spread of experience-based methods of learning, the rapid increase in network affiliation, the autonomous growth of centers and the regional organizations, and a somewhat more controversial development: individuals with more power and influence were coming to NTL for training and consultation. He was less happy that NTL has had so little collaboration or influence in professional schools, except in schools of business administration; that NTL has had little impact in the teaching of the behavioral sciences except through its own network; and that NTL has not had much influence on solutions to current social problems.

Apparently, the new centers will become the core of the NTL operation. At the same time, NTL is giving up its informal accrediting and moving more into consultation, research, and social-action programs focused on special problems such as educational leadership. Such development of centers may move away from regional development to national interests coordinated through a center which could be organized by a group of concerned applied behavioral science practitioners. Emphasis on the more traditional, one-time, laboratory experience probably will decline, and continuing development programs will become more usual.

In 1964, Bradford, Gibb, and Benne (1964a) edited a book which attempted to describe the philosophy, rationale, and general development of laboratory training, and the T-group in particular, and bring together seventeen years of experience. By 1966, it was in its fourth printing, but it is probably not unfair to say that it has never reached a large audience nor has it had the impact it deserves. Since then, there have been increasing attempts to present the history and effects of these two related technologies and to compare them with other group experiences. Because so many people have been attracted as participants, more and more articles are being written which attempt to inform the reader about some of the background and present practices of group experiences (Birnbaum, 1969; Klaw, 1961; Odiorne, 1963; Rakstis, 1970). In particular, there has been an attempt to compare and contrast laboratory experiences with group psychotherapy, and potential participants sometimes are given grave warnings about the danger of the former (Cranshaw, 1969; Kuehn and Crinella, 1969). Statistics which have become available do not appear to support the idea that there is a great danger in training groups (House, 1967a; Lubin and Eddy, 1970). It has been estimated that less than 1 percent of the participants have had serious difficulties which could be related to their group experience (Seashore, 1970). More careful gathering of data is in progress and may help answer the question better for all kinds of group experiences.

As the demand for small group experiences continues, and as more and more practitioners appear and the variety of options increases, it has become inceasingly important, particularly to the two groups of professionals most involved—laboratory trainers and group therapists—to try to clarify their objectives (Gottschalk and Pattison, 1969; Lubin and Eddy, 1970; Pariloff, 1970; Peck and Scheidlinger, 1954; Yalom, 1970).

A danger that is rarely, if ever, warned against, however, is one the authors wish to reemphasize: the danger is that the values which these reeducation innovations were intended to preserve will be lost as the technology is coopted by those who do not understand that "a T-group is more than a technology . . . It has its roots in a system of values relative to mature, productive, and right relationships among people. It is grounded in assumptions about human nature, human learning, and human change. Part of its meaning stems from the commitment of its practitioners to a set of educational goals—both personal and social" (Bradford and others, 1964c, p. 1).

In still another context, Bradford concludes an article on the biography of an institution (on the occasion of its twentieth anniversary): "With the growing recognition on almost all fronts of the speed with which the many kinds of revolutions are sweeping the world, there is real hope that an institution committed to the use of knowledge and methods relevant to the solving of human, organizational, and social problems will grow in ability and usefulness" (Bradford, 1967, p. 143).

Obviously, the training method has been experimenting with a variety of developments and has sought to encompass a broad spectrum of such experiments; however, the NTL Institute seems to have come back to clearly affirming its historical purpose in this statement: "The overriding purpose of NTL Institute is constructive societal change. Its programs focus on the development of individual and organizational dynamics to help create organizations that continually promote both personal and social growth" (NTL Institute, 1970b, p. 4).

The founders of the first laboratory were concerned that people could not deal effectively with the rapid changes forced upon them by the advance of science through technology. They saw the human relations training laboratory as a place where people might be reeducated in order to be more integrated and also as a place to bring about change in the larger social structures. They recognized that everyone needs to participate in many interacting groups, and they wanted to bring them together to collaborate on solutions for social problems: men and women from education, research, and social action who could then act as change agents and be able to help others to cope with change and conflict. Three central values held by these men were the scientific ethic, the democratic ethic, and the importance of the helping relationship, that is, the work of change agents in a problem-solving (collaborative and educational) model.

To do this effectively they looked to many resources for theory and method: to social and behavioral sciences, particularly to Lewin and his theoretical contributions from the field of group dynamics; and in philosophy to people like John Dewey and R. Bruck Raup—again theorists who wished to combine democratic and scientific values. They also looked to social practitioners in the areas of work conferences, leadership training, group psychotherapy, and so forth, for methodology. Over the years, in typical interdisciplinary and interprofessional inclusiveness, they looked for, and accepted influence from, theorists and practitioners of organizational change and individual change. They had very early added the clinical model to the action research model. As we have seen, this attempt to be inclusive often led to an uneasy coexistence rather than to an integrated collaboration. And the time has come for reassessment: is this, as Gottschalk and Pattison (1969) ask, a true new profession? There must be real resolution of objectives through confronting differences and defining the commonalities more systematically.

From the foregoing historical discussion we easily can find a number of issues that press for solution. Bradford and others (1964c) enumerated four problem areas that they predicted would be important for the future of laboratory education: (1) professionalization of trainers, (2) extensions and modifications of T-group method, (3) extended use of the laboratory method in nonlaboratory settings, and (4) expansion of research and theory development. We now can turn to a consideration of these issues.

Early staff members were professionals. At that time, hopefully, the three-week Basic Skills Training Group could train change agents, and the objectives they outlined reflected this intention. However, it soon became apparent that this could not be done in such a short period of time, since most participants did not come with sufficient backgrounds. Obviously, the rapid increase in demand for group experiences (as evidenced by increasing participants and rapidly growing centers and numbers of individuals offering group experiences) has led to a situation where all kinds of *trainers* with varying kinds of preparation and motivation respond to meet the demand and, perhaps, help to create it. This situation will be dealt with later. In 1973, however, an organization to accredit trainers was designed and set in motion. It is called the International Association for Applied Social Scientists.

The training issue will surely be strongly debated if not decided in the next few years. Many individuals have a great deal at stake. At the Third New England Conclave for Applied Behavioral Scientists, held in New Hampshire Jan. 24, 1969, 300 individuals from that region registered for a meeting to discuss ethics and accreditation. Primarily, their concern was with how accreditation might restrict practice, but many participants also expressed a very real desire for further training and supervision which was, and is, largely going unmet everywhere: there must be some way for entry into the "profession" if the quality of practice is to be improved.

We suggest that there should be local and regional opportunities to insure colleagueship, training, and continued education and experience for those already in the field, as well as for those wanting to be in the field. In addition, professionalization may allow the academician theorist/researcher to cooperate more so the field will profit further.

Professionalization efforts ought not to be simply in reaction to what are often "bogeyman" criticisms which suggest that T-groups belong in an *illness* (that is, therapy) rather than a *growth* (that is, education) model, or compare them with week-end entertainments. Rather, it is necessary to help differentiate encounter and therapy groups from T-groups so that both participants and practitioners can find the appropriate model for their objectives. Not all three to six million people (Harris, 1970) who have had group experiences were looking for a T-group, and not all leaders of those groups were offering a T-group. One problem is to match client needs and expectations with trainer competence and objectives.

Apparently, we need to find criteria for selection and training, and at this time for deselection. Again, the issue of training objectives must be faced. One must remember that this was, and is, an educational and reeducational enterprise based on a set of values. It was, and is, also firmly rooted in the social and behavioral sciences. Trainers and potential trainers ought therefore to have a clear understanding of these values; they should be able to model them in their behavior, be skilled in creating a learning environment conducive to these new learnings, and be able to conceptualize and articulate the objectives of their training program.

They will need, therefore, to be relatively conflict-free personally and have some knowledge and appreciation of related theory and research. They will need to recognize the ethical implications of their practices and be concerned with more than technical competence and "gut level" proof of their efforts. They will need to be aware of being related to a body of knowledge, a set of values, and a group of colleagues. As a corollary, training programs should be developed to meet the needs of those seeking to enter the profession and/or to improve their present professional development. In some ways, one of the most difficult and persisting dilemmas has been: how the field can remain inclusive and experimental and yet not lose the very meaning of the T-group and the laboratory. Again, this dilemma began with the inclusion of the clinical personal-integration orientation and emphasis added to the social-psychological action-research orientation of the very early staff at NTL.

At one extreme the development has led to the therapy for normals (*personal growth*) branch as represented by the Western Training Laboratory. It has become difficult to distinguish such groups from encounter groups and group therapy; indeed, they do not want to emphasize the distinction. In this case, the conceptual objectives and the commitment to changing institutions and organizations have largely been given up. According to Weschler, Massarik, and Tannenbaum (1962), they have come to believe that it is more important to deal with individual dynamics than with group dynamics, and they are primarily concerned with freeing the individual from his role-related behaviors and moving him toward personal authenticity. The trainer, and the personality of the trainer, are very important in such a group; and they readily acknowledge that this kind of sensitivity training is closely related to psychotherapy. Many groups, calling themselves T-groups or sensitivity groups, have taken on this orientation without openly identifying themselves as therapy and without the trainers always recognizing the responsibility over time which accompanies a therapeutic approach, as well as the training and supervised experience needed for themselves. In any case, the major focus here is on the intrapersonal and interpersonal relationships of the participants and not on their engagement in action projects. Its purpose is to meet the long-range personal growth needs of the individual participants.

This important development meets the intentions of some trainers/therapists and undoubtedly many participants who seek such experience. It still must be distinguished from other group experiences, such as T-groups, whose focus is on social action or organizational development; and trainers and participants should know that meaningful group experiences and personal growth depend on more than dramatic emotional encounters and attractive

technologies. Still, increased awareness of self and more meaningful interpersonal relations are important goals, and the work of
Bugental and Tannenbaum (1963) and others is important. Also,
however, the problem of transfer of learnings still needs to be
addressed directly for such experiences if the quality of life is to be
changed more than momentarily and if this way of being is to have
some meaning outside artificially created groups.

Another direction for development is the instrumented
laboratory where the trainer's presence has been given up. This
movement is best represented by Blake and his associates (Blake
and Mouton, 1962), and the Southwest Human Relations Training
Laboratory. The first fully instrumented laboratory dates from
1959; eventually it was renamed the *D-group* (development
group). In the T-group, the trainer, through his interventions,
establishes the feedback model. In a D-group, this is accomplished
through various measures and scales—rating scales, check lists, and
rankings—(instruments) which members respond to and which
then are charted and posted. Direct feedback is given by members
as they learn how to use the instruments and interpret them.

Blake and Mouton and their associates believe that D-
groups effect transfer of learnings better than do T-groups, regarding the D-group as an action-research model where participants
can learn about what is going on in their groups by analysis, data
gathering, and evaluation—something they can also do back home.
The staff provide the instruments, and training in their use, and
also can arrange for intergroup exercises and other learning opportunities. They also may use general sessions for various purposes.
They do not sit, however, in the small group, modeling and relating
in ways whereby the participants can experience them as "unique
members" whose special awareness, attitudes, knowledge, and
reactions can be shared and who can be regarded as role models.

Another form of the leaderless group, more closely allied
to the personal growth group, is the *programmed laboratory* where
a series of taped programs is available for self-directed, small groups.
For example, Betty Berzon and her associates formerly at the
Western Behavioral Sciences Institute, developed PEER: Planned
Experiences for Effective Relating. They report that participants
"who went through PEER groups experienced a positive change in

their self-concept while (no-group)' control subjects showed no change in their self-concept over the same period" (Berzon, Reisel, and Davis, 1969). They suggest that there can be promising custom-designed programs in the future: that is, programs to be developed for particular groups of people with a common special concern.

Gibb (1972) has offered a classification of the range of activities that he calls *human relations training* which includes nine "treatments" ranging from "therapy-like" to "education-like": creativity-growth, marathon, emergent, authenticity, sensitivity, programmed, microexperience, inquiry, and embedded. He describes six frequently stated objectives in the training literature for these nine kinds of groups: sensitivity, managing feelings, managing motivations, functional attitudes toward self (for example, self-esteem), functional attitudes toward others (for example, reduced prejudice), and interdependence behavior (for example, inter-personal competence), and claims "promising evidence" that these objectives are met.

In Europe, little has been done in the area of personal growth laboratories. Rather, much group work is related to the issues of work and authority, as represented by Harold Bridges and Gurth Higgin at Tavistock. However, two interesting developments which may effect practitioners in the United States are related to the activities of Roger Harrison in England and Gunnar Hjelholt in Denmark. Harrison is developing *autonomy laboratories,* and Hjeholt is working with small communities which are set up temporarily. Both emphasize providing the resources required but not imposing staff designs on the participants. Instead, the partici-pants are responsible for their own learning by making whatever use of the resources they wish. This indicates an important step forward in the development of true shared leadership.

Obviously it is important that participants know more clearly what kind of group experience they are going to share in, and trainers need to know what the objectives of each of the variants of group practice are and which they are going to work towards. Participants' expectations and trainers' intentions need to be as explicit as possible if group experiences are to be productive and appropriate.

A study by Lieberman and Gardner (1973) compares

persons attending growth centers, persons in therapy, and those attending NTL laboratories. One of their striking findings concerns the expectations of these different groups. "NTL participants share with clinic patients a perception that change involves some painful and anxiety-producing moments. They see as an important part of the process discovering undesirable or unacceptable things about themselves, being confronted and challenged, at times becoming anxious or depressed, and experiencing strong negative feelings or expressing them. . . . It is the avoidance of the painful aspects that most characterizes the distinctive processs expectation of the growth center participants from both NTL and clinic patients. The growth center people do not expect to have more joy or positive feelings than the NTL people; it is just that they have an ordered set of expectations that systematically excludes painful experiences in the change process" (pp. 2–3).

Originally, training groups were "stranger groups" in "island settings," that is, individuals came from a variety of places, occupations, and organizations to a secluded place for an extended period of time. This was done on theoretical grounds, that is, as offering conditions conducive to attitude change. Thus the emphasis was on removing or reducing restraining forces which prevent change. Now we need to look again to theory and research for hypotheses about how to use these technologies in system interventions, and so forth, which do not take people away to some new setting and which use people who work together and know each other. Obviously, there would be more restraining forces, at least at the start, but transfer of training from the laboratory to the work situation and other real life situations would seem to be favored by team development (Kuriloff and Atkins, 1966), organizational development (Shepard, 1965), and other related programs in such environments as industry, government, the schools and higher education, as well as communal living arrangements. These settings could include a tenants' organization in a low-income housing project, the staff of a hospital unit, a college dormitory, a model city program, a drug drop-in center, a consumers' cooperative, and so forth.

Again, we must reconsider the question of the objectives of T-group and laboratory training when we think of the extended use of the laboratory method: are participants to be change agents? As Albee (1970) says in regard to clinical psychology: the three important issues to attack for improving the quality of life are racism, sexism, and the destructive effects of the profit motive. A number of people in the laboratory training profession at large, and within the NTL network as well, probably agree that this is equally true for their field and want to attack these social issues. Recent developments in the NTL organization around the idea of centers may be moving in this direction if these centers become foci for theorists-researchers-consultants and trainers to work together around important issues with a wider variety of people.

The early commitment in laboratory training was to social change, it will be recalled, and the training of change agents, necessitating planned change efforts which were accomplished within the framework of on educational model based on a new collaborative style of problem-solving. A *laissez-faire* theory of change assumes that things work themselves out if left alone. A *radical intervention* theory of change assumes that changes must be forced. A *planned change* approach, such as the laboratory approach, recognizes the T-group as an important instrument for, and vehicle for, change efforts.

The self-renewal of all systems is a necessity, as Gardner reminds us so eloquently (Gardner, 1965, 1969). This is true for individuals, groups, and organizations, and it is necessary for all systems to build in ways of self-renewal. However, society does not ordinarily encourage such activities; indeed it often stands in the way. So these innovative educational approaches, the T-group and the laboratory, are ways of learning how to make significant interventions in the system. How this can be done effectively needs further experimentation and evaluation of efforts. It does appear, however, as if it will become more and more appropriate to work with family groups rather than with stranger groups if the outcomes of T-group and laboratory training are to be transferred meaningfully and if action is to result from training. This will mean working with people who work together and perhaps live together, and it will involve more extended training programs. These groups may be more or less permanent or temporary. Bennis quotes De Tocqueville who said: "I am tempted to believe that what we call necessary institutions are often no more than institutions to which we have become accustomed. In matters of social constitution, the field of possibilities is much more extensive than men living in their various societies are ready to imagine" (Bennis, 1968a, p. 76)'.

Given the present state of flux, Bennis then goes on later to say for himself that we need an educational system that can "help us make a virtue out of contingency rather than one which induces hesitancy or its reckless companion, expedience" (Bennis, 1968b, p. 127). Such a system would develop at least the following inter-personal competencies: "(1) learning how to develop intense and deep human relationships quickly—and learning how to 'let go' . . . ; (2) learning how to enter groups and leave them; (3) learning what roles are satisfying and how to attain them; (4) learning how to widen the repertory of feelings and roles available; (5) learning how to cope more readily with ambiguity; (6) learning how to develop a strategic comprehensibility of a new 'culture' or system and what distinguishes it from other cultures; and finally (7) learning how to develop a sense of one's uniqueness" (Bennis, 1968b, pp. 127–128).

Not so incidentally, Bennis and Slater (1968) emphasize that in this new world of "the temporary society" individuals will need a greater fidelity to something or someone in order to be more fully human. Bennis suggests this might be a marriage partner or an organization or a group. Slater points out that there may be the equivalent of "serial monogamy" in relation to a group or a partner: total commitment to a single group (and/or partner) for a limited time. All of these "predictions" seem to support the idea that T-groups and laboratories (which are places where temporary groups can be experienced and understood) are important places for many kinds of learnings to be worked on. And they provide an opportunity during this present transition period when old forms are breaking up and new ones are forming for experimentation with understanding.

All of these questions point to a real need for theoretical bases and for research support to help conceptualize what these technologies, the T-group and the laboratory, can do; how this need relates to the important metagoals of the T-group and laboratory approach; and how effective they are as training methods, that is, for transfer of learnings. The present condition of T-group theory, research, and practice can be rather vividly described by analogy: it is a little like giving a concert performance at the same time that the concert hall is being built, the music is being written, the instruments are being produced, the musicians are still rehearsing, and the conductor is making his debut.

In 1964, Gibb (1964a) described the status of T-group theory at that time. Not too much has changed since then; although technology can make great strides overnight, science still must plod along, accruing its insights painstakingly. In addition, by now there are probably at least 100 practitioners for every researcher, and, many researchers do not work out of a theoretical frame of reference so that application continues to outstrip integration at an increasing rate. As Gibb so rightly points out, "In education, therapy and training, as in other engineering fields, practice tends to outstrip theory. Practice is refined from a series of gradualistic innovations which grow out of some blending of miniature models, intuitive impressions, empirical data, opportunistic considerations, and systematic thinking" (Gibb, 1964a, p. 168).

That there is nothing so practical as a good theory is a proverbial statement attributed to Kurt Lewin. Three of the critical functions which any theory can serve are: (1) selective: that is, to help someone choose a problem; (2) heuristic: that is, to lead to experimentation; (3) illuminative: that is, to help clarify meaning.

Gibb (1964a, p. 170) summarizes how these three functions can be useful for four classes of recipients: theorist, researcher, trainer, and participant, and the reader may wish to identify with one or all of these recipients.

In many fields, practice, research, and theory have little influence on each other. It would seem more likely, and highly desirable, that there be much more cross influence in the area of T-group theory, research, and practice since applied behavioral scientists are engaged in all three areas. Because practice continues and expands, it has come to bring pressure on theorists and researchers to offer clarification and testable hypotheses. Thus as Gibb says of the theories in Bradford and others, these are "rationalizations of practices that are growing up in a rapidly expanding field of professional activity" (Bradford and others, 1964a, pp. 184–

185). However, the fact that T-group theory cannot adequately offer an elegant theory of behavior change is also a commentary on the state of behavioral science theory in general.

Gibb, in his sympathetic but hard-hitting critique, listed some "unfinished tasks" for the theorist which are still important questions to think about and act on, although some constructive work has been done in the meantime:

(1) *Integration of theory and data from the behavioral sciences:* The very fact that the field has been interdisciplinary and interprofessional—which is one of its unique strengths—also has resulted in the lack of "a unified theory of behavior-change—in group phenomena"—and this integration is still to be done.

(2) *The experiential nature of T-group training:* Again there is a dilemma—the theorists are also practitioners and this keeps the face validity of their writing high. However a theory that will be useful to theorists and researchers needs to meet some of the more traditional requirements of theorizing and validation. "This criterion is a severe one for engineering theories of education, therapy, training, and child rearing. To a significant degree, such theory *is* embedded in the therapist, trainer, and parent—and appropriately and necessarily so."

(3) *Vulnerability to Empirical Test:* There is little entry into direct testing of the "theories" presented in Bradford and little attempt to tie it to existing research. This is left to the reader.

(4) *Dynamics of the Learning Process:* Again a strength becomes a weakness: here is a valid theory of group experience, but so little is done about the dynamics of the learning process in the person. "It is unfortunate for each of the three areas that there is so little cross-fertilization among the three fields of traditional learning theory, the psychodynamics of personality, and the dynamics of in-a-group learning."

(5) *Diversity and Power of Constructs:* To have a complete T-group theory would mean to have a complete social science theory. Instead there is an inclusive use of constructs, but no attempt to provide a "road map"—just a lot of territory.

(6) *The Art and the Science:* To acknowledge that to lead a T-group requires "artistic, intuitive, technological, professional, scientific, and highly personal elements" can also be a cop-out.

"Science will eventually contribute much more to the technology, and technology much more to the art." [Gibb, 1964a, adapted from pp. 185–189].

At that time, the following theoretical issues were discussed: (1) Membership and the Learning Process (Bradford, 1964); (2) From Polarization to Paradox (Benne, 1964b); (3) Patterns and Vicissitudes in T-group Development (Bennis, 1964); (4) Climate for Trust Formation (Gibb, 1964b); (5) Psychodynamic Principles Underlying T-group Processes (Whitman, 1964); (6) Studying Group Action (Blake, 1964); (7) Training in Conflict Resolution (Horwitz, 1964a); (8) Explorations in Observant Participation (Shepard, 1964). Each was offered by a practitioner-theorist; each contribution is mainly to the *selective* function of theory-building. At that time, few studies cited in the Stock chapter (Stock, 1964, pp. 395–441) summarizing research up to that time were related to these emerging T-group theories.

Posing theoretical questions and presenting theoretical analyses should lead others to test these and perhaps go further with them mathematically, deductively, or through other logical processes, to test the constructs and relationships. Such effort is accomplished through some of the analyses presented by the writers mentioned in the previous paragraph. For example, Gibb's (1964b) formulations about the differences between the persuasive model of group functioning and the participative model leads readily and insistently to the testing out of the implications. Taken all together, these theorists show particularly strong interests in the structure and functions of the small group; other problems will need attention from other theorists while more comprehensive theories are being constructed.

Buchanan (1969) updates theoretical developments since the Bradford book (1964). He finds three foci: how an individual learns in T-groups, processes of planned organizational development, and processes of group development. Among those he cites who have contributed to a theoretical understanding of how an individual learns in T-groups are: Hampden-Turner (1966), Harrison (1969), Argyris (1964), Clark and Culbert (1965), Schein and Bennis (1965), and P. B. Smith (1967). Several other theorists have written about organizations showing how laboratory training is consistent with and can be useful to organizational goals: (Bennis, 1966; Davis, 1967; McGregor, 1960; Schein and Bennis, 1965; Shepard, 1965).

In order to move from theory to research, testable statements must be formulated. Practitioners often make their decisions expediently or impressionistically: for example, who shall be in a group; what style of trainer interventions will be used, and so forth. Research, if it is more closely tied to practice than theory, will therefore also be expedient, and the long arduous process of testing hypotheses and modifying theory will not make much progress. We recommend that all trainers give heed to the relationship between what they are doing and how to conceptualize the rationale, the processes, and the outcomes. Since theory gives license to practitioners by providing a foundation for what they do, it should therefore be able to expect some reciprocity. This point of view will be discussed at greater length in the chapter on training. Actually, innovations in T-groups have developed largely through practice rather than from theory or research. But there has not been enough cross-fertilization: the pieces need to be put together to make a clearer picture.

Certainly social psychology and personality theory can contribute to T-group theory, as do theories about influence: for example, from therapy, counseling, and so forth. However, "A barrier to such reciprocal influence is the diversity of clinical and empirical literature using different terminologies, different operations for independent variables, and widely varying language systems for communicating results" (Gibb, 1964a, p. 178).

For the trainer, theory helps him focus on what is going on (a selective function); it allows him to have more options and to test out his behaviors as hypotheses (a heuristic function); and: "The trainer might hope that a training theory would put things in such perspective as to help him arrive at a theory that would fit his understandings of the whole body of knowledge in the behavioral and social sciences, and somehow synthesize his own value system and ontology with this body of knowledge. Because the trainer invests so much of his person in the process of interaction in the T-group, it is perhaps more necessary that he make this synthesis than that the therapist, educator or parent do so" (Gibb, 1964a, p. 181). The participant also can use theory: to help him look at certain parts of his experience, to help him experiment and assess the results, and to help him understand and conceptualize so there can be more integrative experiences for him.

Research can be an important link between theory and practice, and indeed the model of the trainer-researcher would probably do much to correct the imbalance of theorist-to-practitioner ratio. Without such a model, connections between theory and practice are largely nonexistent except in rare instances. Even the link between researcher and theorist is so tenuous that much research appears to be strictly empirical in nature and does little to add to a cumulative body of knowledge, again except for a small number of investigators. Some order, however, has been brought to bear upon these scattered researchers by those who have chosen to review the available research literature from time to time. Each has chosen his or her set of categories for the task, which represents in some way the expectations put on studies by the reviewer.

There are, of course, difficult methodological problems and rather inelegant available theories which make it a formidable undertaking to attempt significant research in the area of T-groups and laboratory training. Harrison (1969) has made an important contribution to work in this area, to be discussed at length in Chapter Four. He has defined some critical methodological problems (such as the issue of control groups) and has tried to suggest solutions which would encourage investigation of important questions.

Meanwhile, let us turn to three major reviews [see also Durham and others (1967)], beginning with the first review of the literature by Stock 1964. Stock took on the task of trying to bring some order to the often unrelated individual studies that had been carried out previously. She grouped these studies in seven categories: (1) the course of development in the T-group; (2) group composition; (3) the character of the T-group as described by members; (4) the role of the trainer in the T-group; (5) individual behavior in the T-group; (6) members' perceptions of each other; and (7) the impact of the T-group on individual learning and change. As can be seen, there is little or no emphasis on transfer-ability of learnings; already practice had come a long way from Lewin's attitude change studies in 1953.

After reviewing these studies, Stock invites the reader to finish the sentence "Why doesn't somebody study . . . ?" She points out that there were (and are) many important questions yet unanswered, and indeed, yet unasked. Identifying trends in research, or projecting trends, for that period of time seemed to be difficult tasks, but she did venture to say: "In general there appears to be a shift toward emphasizing research which is rather specifically relevant to training and has simultaneous implications for applica-tion and theory. At the same time, there appears to be a more consistent interest in developing and testing theory which may be relevant to the functioning and impact of the T-group" (Stock, 1964, p. 437). There were, of course, two important factors to be considered when looking at the research picture. One, the rather common problem of the limitations imposed by inadequate meth-odology. As Stock points out, curiosity often outstrips methodology, but researchers often are bound by what is available. Still there was an indication that measures were being invented and utilized with some success, a trend that has continued.

A second factor in considering the lack of programmatic research concerned the role of NTL vis-a-vis research. There was no question about support for the idea of research, but there were some real problems about the primacy of training versus research. One solution appeared to be to integrate the research into the training design (for example, feedback sessions that are part of the training design and part of the research design), and perhaps to develop the trainer-researcher model discussed earlier. More ideally there would be the development of trainer-researcher-theorist teams.

Campbell and Dunnette (1968) examined the utility of T-group experiences for managerial training and development. They were careful to identify themselves as academic psychologists, not practitioners, and their review reflects this critical stance. Their major focus is on transferability of learnings to the organization, and thus they look to external criteria, that is, those linked directly with job behavior. However, they also take into account internal criteria, that is, measures linked to the training program itself (for example, before-and-after-training attitude change) but not linked to the goals of the organization. Both external and internal criteria are considered relevant to an understanding of transferability of learning from T-group to organization. Their criticism is largely based on their interest in judging the relative usefulness of T-group training as a personnel development technique. Further, they are rightly critical of the methodological shortcomings in the field, although they do acknowledge the difficulties of observation and measurement in this area. However, they also question the nature and viability of the assumptions they see as underlying T-group training (for example, that anxiety is a necessary condition for learning). And not unexpectedly they challenge the T-group method to demonstrate its usefulness—which they believe has not been done. Indeed they are more inclined to accept it as "aesthetic appreciation or recreational enjoyment" rather than have "existential" orientation confused with what they define as "scientific" orientation.

Thus they try to identify and summarize the crucial elements of the T-group method, call attention to some of the difficulties in researching the dynamics and effects of the method, and summarize the research evidence bearing on the utility of T-groups for training and development purposes. They conclude that: (1) The evidence, though limited, is reasonably convincing that T-group training does induce behavioral changes in the back-home setting, that is, that "group differences have been obtained which seem to be compatible with some of the major objectives of laboratory training" (Campbell and Dunnette, 1968, pp. 98–99). (2) The results with internal criteria are more numerous but even less conclusive. However, they do recommend how research should proceed: (1) Researchers must devote more effort to specifying the behavioral outcomes they expect to observe as a result of T-group training. (2) More measures of individual differences must be incorporated in future T-group studies. (3) More attention must be given to interactions between organizational characteristics, leadership climates, organizational goals, and training outcomes and effects. (4) The effects of T-group training should be compared more fully with the behavioral effects stemming from other training methods. (5) A corollary to the above is the need to explore the *interaction* of

T-group training and other learning experiences. (6) It is imperative that the relative contributions of various technological elements in the T-group method be more fully understood. (7) Finally, more effort should be directed toward forging the link between training-induced behavior changes and changes in job-performance effectiveness (Campbell and Dunnette, 1968, pp. 99–100).

In summary, Campbell and Dunnette point out that there is little evidence that T-group training has positive utility for organizations but do not deny that there may be utility for the individual. In this connection, they point out the danger of confusing existential and scientific orientations, leaving it to the individual to decide if an experience is "life-enhancing" but reminding us that normative data are required for scientific purposes. They conclude that "for the time being, the T-group must remain a very interesting and challenging research area, which is where the energies of its proponents should be applied" (Campbell and Dunnette, 1968, p. 101).

When, in 1969, Buchanan brought up to date an earlier review of laboratory literature (including T-groups), he concluded: (1) Laboratory training is effective as a means of facilitating specifiable changes in individuals in the industrial setting. (2) It has been used effectively in some programs of organizational development, but not in others. (3) Behavioral scientists associated with the National Training Laboratories are actively engaged in subjecting their theories and methods to systematic analysis, and in developing strategies for organization development. (4) Some of these strategies, now being studied systematically, are showing exciting results (Buchanan, 1969, p. 466). At the theoretical level, House (1967b) generates a paradigm for looking at relationships among input variables (methods of inducing change), output variables (objectives of training), and intervening variables (initial state of participant and organization) which allows us to look at any change in the "person dimension." Harrison (1969) takes some specific methodological issues and suggests ways for dealing with them. Miles (1965) uses a method called "the clinical-experimental approach" which involves a set of researchers separate from the practitioners. Each makes predictions: the researchers from a point of view of theory, the practitioners as change agents using an action/research orientation. Data are collected clinically (running account) and experimentally (preplanned schedule), and the design is assessed tactically as well.

Perhaps most encouraging is the fact that more people are beginning to try to offer some integrating ideas which can be tested. But there are still many questions: for example, what is the nature of the relationship between the training and the outcome, theoretically; what can be said about the theoretical connection between change and transfer of learning; if laboratory training is part of a larger organization development program, how designate what part is due to the laboratory, and so forth? All in all, there still is much work to be done methodologically before research results are useful. Buchanan concludes that answers to the questions about the usefulness of laboratory training and what kind of laboratory training provides useful concepts and skills for organizational development must come from theories about effective organization functioning, not from outcomes of programs. He suggests that: "Blake and Mouton (1964) have made a case for laboratory training based on grid theory; Shepard (1965), Likert (1967), Argyris (1964), Bennis (1966) and McGregor (1960) have provided relevant theory in the case of non-grid laboratory training; and Miles (1965) has systematically sought empirical data relevant to the question as it pertains to school systems (Buchanan, 1969, p. 477). He concludes his very detailed analysis of current research with a modest set of summary statements about the value of laboratory training: (1) It facilitates personal growth and development, and thus can be of value to the individual who participates. (2) It accomplishes changes in individuals which according to several theories are important in effecting change in organizations and in effectively managing organizations. (3) One study, in which an instrumented laboratory was compared with sensitivity training, provides some indication that more organizational change resulted from the instrumented approach. (4) The findings from this literature search are compatible with the conclusions reached in a similar review made four years ago (Buchanan, 1969, p. 477).

In summarizing the results of 106 studies reviewed in terms of their stated training objectives, Gibb (1972) concludes there are some promising theories, some meager data, and some methodological innovations; yet there are no adequate tests of theories of group growth. Thus it is difficult to talk about the power of training designs or leader interventions leading to behavior change. After examining the nine "treatments" (kinds of groups), he finds the methods promising but says that there is little hard evidence for behavior change. Four variables that do seem to be important and warrant further study are: composition of the group, feedback, leader behavior, and duration of training. He concludes with a set of "conservative implications" in which he calls for cross-fertilization of treatments and experimentation with methods; he suggests that feedback and feeling expression are important, effects of the trainer are important, training embedded in long-range programs is desirable, heterogeneity of groups seems desirable, and research efforts can be integrated into training aims. It is an optimistic report of the effects of human relations training, broadly defined, and based on "promising evidence."

From the beginning, it was hoped and intended that the training laboratory would link action, education, and behavioral research. Research may also be the link between practice and theory, in all directions. It has been held back until now by a number of barriers. Among these are: the assumption that there is a conflict between research needs and training needs (this seems to be getting resolved as more imaginative designs are evolved and participants are taken into the total designs as collaborators); and, traditionally, laboratories have been brief and nonrecurring, and follow-up studies have required much time and money (this situation can probably be alleviated as there is more collaboration with university-based research and as more nonstranger laboratories and programs are begun). The new NTL Centers may also stimulate and support more programmatic research.

It seems very important to begin to research the assumptions underlying the T-group and the laboratory technologies. Some of these assumptions have been articulated by Buchanan (1969); Campbell and Dunnette (1968); Golembiewski and Blumberg (1970); Lubin and Eddy (1970). If such research has begun already, then theoretical formulations will have some opportunity to be verified and perhaps modified, and practitioners and participants will have an opportunity to add to this important process. For example, Campbell and Dunnette offer these as assumptions to be tested: (1) A substantial number of group members, when confronted with others' behaviors and feelings in an atmosphere of psychological safety, can produce articulate and constructive feedback. (2) A significant number of the group members can agree on the major aspects of a particular individual's behavior exhibited in the group situation. Certainly a complete consensus is not to be expected, but neither must the feedback go off in all directions. A certain degree of communality is necessary if the feedback is to be helpful for the individual. (3) Feedback is relatively complete and deals with significant aspects of the individual's behavior. (4) The behavior emitted in the group is sufficiently representative of behavior outside the group so that learning occurring within the group will carry over or transfer. (5) Psychological safety can be achieved relatively quickly (in the matter of a few hours) among either complete strangers or among associates who have had varying types and degrees of interpersonal interaction. (6) Almost everyone initially lacks interpersonal competence; that is, individuals tend to have distorted self-images, faulty perceptions, and poor communication skills. (7) Anxiety facilitates new learning. (8) Finally, transfer of training occurs between the cultural island and the 'back-home' situation (Campbell and Dunnette, 1968, p. 77).

The T-group is a development in the technology of education based on a system of values. It can be viewed moreover as an experimental paradigm for a new kind of functional community group. Furthermore, it belongs integrally in a setting, for example, the human relations training laboratory which can be seen as a kind of organization. Thus it is a way of establishing a learning environment which assumes a problem-solving approach to human relations problems, and to personal and organizational change, around three values: the scientific ethic, the democratic ethic, and the help-sharing relationship as represented by the change agent.

It needs to look to scientists for theoretical foundations, to researchers for verification and modification, to practitioners for implementation, and to participants for action. But how does it work?

For that we can look to Chapter Four which tries to elaborate a view of human nature which has increasing theoretical support and give some picture of what happens in a T-group—a place where people can change, can create a new kind of world, and can then go back to try to change the old one.

not be accomplished by a ritual incantation requiring a few choice sentences at the beginning of the first meeting hour. This is not because the members must learn how to relate in the nuclear family —it is because of the resistance that each individual has against interacting in a situation that will mobilize within him ineffectual patterns of interaction and painful thoughts and feelings.

Creating a structure involves giving shape and direction to that which was first formless. The house that springs up in the formerly empty meadow is created from a floor plan, made real by concrete and 2 by 4's through the active intervention of a number of carpenters. The group also may start out as a formless entity; it will not, however, remain so for long. As soon as the members congregate, they will, in the absence of the therapist, try to impose upon the group their own form and directions. Alternative plans will be brought forth by group members. They will pose the questions: "How shall we behave?" "Shall we be an interest group?" "Shall we be a tea party; Mrs. Jones will be responsible for the cookies." "Shall we be an activity group or a discussion group?"

Clearly, members arrive with a number of plans and an eagerness to implement them. These are structures that may be suggested in the absence of the therapist; upon his arrival the group may come up with additional structures designed specifically to accommodate him. For example, a group of out-patients coming to the Veterans Administration medical office in Miami, Florida, for psychotherapy have greeted the author, as therapist, with what can best be paraphrased as "You are the Doctor and these are our symptoms, cure us." A group of college students on academic probation have greeted him with a still different structure. They state, "You are the group counselor, an agent of the college; here are the names of the teachers who have harassed us; do something to change this situation which is ruining our academic careers." Generally, the structural planning of the group, if left to the members, will include the therapist, and as can be seen by the two previous illustrations, will be formulated so that their expectations of the therapist will be defined by their perceptions of his institutional role. In the case of private practice where the therapist does not carry any institutionally-assigned role, the members will perceive him in the traditional role of the healer.

The therapist, however, is the architect of the group. It is his job to communicate his floor plan to them and then to see that this floor plan remains the model which governs the form and direction of the group from its inception to its conclusion. And the model involves a temporary reconstitution of the nuclear family as mentioned in the introduction. To accomplish this purpose he must initially define both his own role and that of the group. The group is enjoined to talk about whatever they like, and he defines himself as a listener who will comment from time to time on the group's thoughts, feelings, and attitudes.

Throughout the life of the group, it is of utmost importance that the therapist maintains its original structure. The analogy of building a house holds here again. Once the house has been framed, small alterations of the inside design are possible, but the original plan must be adhered to if the structure is to be sound. The group members will continue in their initial sessions to try to force a different structure on the therapist. After deciding upon an alternative plan for their group, they will try over and over again to win the therapist over to their plan; failing, they may become angry and denounce him as at best insensitive and at worst hostile to their best interests. For example, a group of World War II veterans referred to a Veterans Administration psychotherapy group at the V.A. Mental Hygiene Clinic in Miami, Florida, for help with psychosomatic complaints had been told individually before the first meeting that they were there for psychological help and that their therapist was not a physician; nevertheless they used their initial sessions to air their physical complaints to him. When he refused to respond in the traditional manner of a physician, they became angry and accusatory. Through all similar situations, the therapist can do best by adhering to his original communication, namely, defining his role to the group and the behavior he expects the group members to assume to him and to each other.

A major goal of the therapist is to facilitate communication. Satir (1964) defines communication as a verbal and nonverbal process by which a sender makes requests of the receiver. It should be added that the receiver responds to the sender's lead, thereby becoming a sender himself. The original request may be in the form of a declaration or a question. The therapist operates as an alert receiver both of messages sent from patient to patient, from patients to groups, from patients to therapist, and from group to therapist. To accomplish this, the therapist must be able to distinguish between the denotative and the connotative aspects of the statements received. For example, father may be denoted as one who supports the family but connotated as one who is stern and punishing. To understand which of the two examples is being referred to by the patient, the therapist must know something of the history of the patient's revelations in the group, his relationship to the other patients, and above all, both the patient's and the group's relationship to the therapist himself.

The basic direction of communication in the group therapy session is from the group members to the therapist—once it has been established by the therapist's instructions on roles in the group, and especially as conveyed through his directions to the group to talk about whatever they wish. In order that one understands these communications, it is necessary to understand the *transference* phenomenon. Transference is defined by Fenichel (1945, p. 45) as the "repetition of previously acquired attitudes towards the analyst." The phenomenon applies equally well for the term group therapist.

The group therapist will, in effect, become the recipient of previously acquired attitudes of each group member. This point raises a series of major questions: How have the group members acquired these attitudes? How can we speak of communication within a group if each of its members is responding to the therapist on the basis of a uniquely acquired set of attitudes? How does the therapist communicate to a group as opposed to congeries of individuals if each member holds a unique set of transference attitudes? Finally, what is the effect of the presence of several group members on the intensity of the transference, how is this intensity communicated to the therapist, and how does the therapist perceive and respond to such communications?

In answer to the first question of how previous attitudes have become acquired, the reader can be introduced directly into the controversial field of child-rearing, specifically of behavioristic versus nativist theories of human development. Since the material developed in this chapter is based upon a psychoanalytical model of personality development, our basic assumptions permit us to side-step most of the controversy. However, even within the psycho-analytical model itself there are many controversial issues. It is therefore necessary even within this framework to make a further choice. The proposed framework for personality development presented here is taken from the psychoanalytical group who think of themselves as ego psychologists and whose principal theoretician is Erik H. Erikson. Following Erickson's ego psychology (1959, 1962), one would expect those attitudes that will later become part of therapeutic transference to be acquired through attempts at resolution of the three basic conflicts of childhood and the one significant conflict of adolescence. Specifically, these are the con-flicts between trust and mistrust occurring in infancy, between autonomy or shame and doubt occurring at the second year of life, and the conflict of initiative as opposed to guilt, coming sometime between the third and the fifth year of life. Most significant in the late teens is the conflict between identity formation and role diffu-sion. In all of these conflicts, success or failure of resolution is an interpersonal phenomenon. This development takes place through the mutuality between the child and a significant adult who very early in life is usually the mother or mother surrogate, and finally, during the third year, someone must be cast in the role of a father. During the adolescent period, relationships with peers (sibling sur-rogates) and significant adults (parent surrogates) must be broad-ened and recast if a youth is to find his identity, that is, if he is to become a unique individual with his own set of life values and atti-tudes. The working concept that allows for the acquisition of positive attitudes toward mutuality described by Erikson is one that has adaptive qualities or virtues and is called identification.

Through the identification process the infant accepts the consistency of mothering and the virtue of trust. Again, through identification, the toddler accepts socialization of his impulses and his behavior develops along acceptable cultural lines that are mediated by his mother. Having accepted through this process the idea that his desires and his mother's set of appropriate behaviors are the same, he becomes socialized while retaining the illusion of free will or autonomous action. A short time later, through identi-fication with the parent of the same sex, he is able to empathize with and understand his sex appropriate roles and to share in the initiatives of introduction into the learning experiences of his culture.

Finally, through identification with his peers and then with significant adults, he is able to confront the questions: what is the world out there really like, and do I have the capabilities to make my way in this world? Successful confrontation of these questions leads youth to an adult identity, while failure leads at best to a continual unhappy seeking for self into the adult years and, at worst, to a schizophrenic withdrawal into fantasy solutions. Failure of mutuality and, therefore, of identity formation at each conflict level leads not only to lack of resolution and acquisition of the adaptive virtues but also to a continuing need to search for resolution. The low structure of the therapeutic relationship allows for the appearance and intensification of attitudes previously acquired through failure of mutuality. These attitudes will repeat themselves with increasing frequency and intensity, becoming progressively obvious to the therapist, the group members, and finally, to the patient himself.

Having dealt in rather summary form with the acquisition of patient attitudes available for transference, we can now move to the importance of the second question. For if each group member is projecting his own set of attitudes onto the group psychotherapist, how is it possible for the therapist to receive a dozen or so communications of transference attitudes and how is it possible for him to respond? For if he responds, to whom does he respond? At this point, Redl's (1966) concept of contagion can be used with great success to answer these questions.

Contagion is used by Redl as an epidemological term, only here he speaks of the rapid spread from group member to group member of a set of ideas with their accompanying affects. This set of a logically coherent sequence of ideas is called a theme. (See Powdermaker and others, 1953, Winder and Hersko, 1958.) A theme may dominate part or all of a given therapy session and may even extend into several future therapy sessions. The theme always contains transference elements. For example, a theme and its variations dealing with the poor medical services a group member is presently receiving sends the transference message: "You, the therapist, do not care enough to help me, and I may die if abandoned by you." This appears to present a set of attitudes right out of Erikson's first conflict, stating "I did not trust anyone" (specifically, mother) "to adequately feed and hold me." At this point one turns again to the question, why should contagion occur? Why does not the therapist deal only with the individual who has made these statements? The first proof of contagion is that other members, some more enthusiastically, some less, will take up variations on the theme, supporting the original statement or sometimes denying its truth or its relevance. Others may make a strong effort to change the subject, as if they cannot countenance the consideration of this theme by the group. It is this heightened activity revolving about the theme, pro and con, that constitutes major evidence of its importance to all group members. In addition, since all group members experience the developmental conflicts discussed earlier in this chapter, it should not be surprising that all members are more or less concerned both with the present question, will you care for me? and its derivatives from the past, mother never cared adequately enough for me. Therefore, while each patient has uniquely acquired his transference attitudes on the basis of unique experiences with his own parents and siblings, nevertheless each suffers some lack of resolution of all previous conflicts. Each patient is, therefore, compelled to respond either directly or indirectly out of the unresolved conflicts of his past.

Many group therapists raise the issue concerning the effect on the transference phenomena of several patients sharing the therapist's time and attention during group session. There are practitioners who have described the transference as diluted, using the analogy of adding water to a solution, thereby reducing its strength. It would seem, in spite of the writing of many practitioners who have had years of experience with group psychotherapy, that Freud's (1922) group psychotherapy and the analysis of the ego has made the most substantive statement on this problem. His statement on the origins of the "group mind" clearly explains that the quality of transference within a group is acquired by a combined process: the willingness of each individual to surrender his sense of uniqueness and the willingness of group members to act in concert out of their "love for the leader."

More specifically, Freud (1922) likens the transference

occurring in a relatively unstructured group to that occurring in hypnosis. When the hypnotist gives the command to sleep, he is putting himself in the position of one of the subject's parents. In psychoanalytic terminology, the subject has placed the object (the hypnotist) in the place of his ego ideal (the parental image). In the group, a number of individuals have put one and the same object (the group leader) in the place of their ego ideal. The group further adds to the process of hypnosis because the group members have also identified themselves with one another in their egos. Through this process of identification with each other, group members are able to minimize the operation of strong forces of jealousy and envy that would otherwise make working together in the group an impossibility.

It has already been mentioned that the therapist's major function is the facilitation of communication. The context in which he both receives messages from group members and sends his own messages is that of a low structured group, one in which the members are brought together with the knowledge that the task before them commits them to be collaborators in a process of bringing about some internal psychological changes within themselves. It is incumbent upon the therapist to facilitate group interaction with the purpose of bringing about this change.

The therapist is an initiator of responses. To initiate responses the therapist has in mind the dimensions of group interaction, a knowledge of the conflict the group is presently trying to resolve, and a knowledge of the individual character structure of each patient and how this character structure is expressed in the style of the individual group member. With these factors in mind the therapist is now ready to initiate responses. His first rule is to start with the patients. While all patients have arrived with the wish to be helped, and have vocalized this wish, they also have arrived with a desire to maintain their already tried ways of thinking, feeling, and acting and have not vocalized their fear of relinquishing any of these. For example, the patient's great craving at the initial session is to communicate to the therapist in the same statement both the pressure they (patient and therapist) are under, and to request some form of relief. The current cultural means for communicating this is a statement of symptoms, which appears clearly in the following excerpt:

> Therapist: We're in session.
>
> Bill: I'd like to get to know who you all are. If we're going to spend fifteen weeks together we should get to know each other by first name at least.
>
> (Each member began telling his first name.)
>
> Harry: Okay, I'll play games, my name's Jim.
>
> Therapist: Mr. Smith is my recorder.
>
> Frank: I think you said last week that the basic problem was not being able to study? Did you go back to the library and try to study?
>
> Joe: No, nothing much of a change.
>
> Mike: Anyone do any better since last week?
>
> Bill: Not with the tests, but I feel I'm communicating a little better.
>
> Jim: My dorm is too noisy. I've got to get out of there in order to study. My roommate is noisy, but maybe that's an excuse.
>
> Bill: You're not really sure.
>
> Jim: I try to study but he doesn't help me. We begin doing other things.
>
> Frank: Could you switch roommates?
>
> Jim: We're going to try that, maybe.
>
> Frank: Do you get along with him? Do you do things together?
>
> Jim: Yes, we do. That's maybe the problem.
>
> Helen: I feel that you are blaming him and really you feel jealous of him because he is making it. (pause) I feel that you just want to put blame on him.
>
> Jim: Well, I said that this might be an excuse.
>
> Mike: My roommate is terrific.
>
> Frank: Do you think our problem is that it's hard to study? My mind wanders, and I know if I wanted to study I could do it.
>
> George: You always do the things you like to study first. (pause)
>
> Josh: Anybody study an extra half hour last week?
>
> Frank: No, I took a trip to Springfield. Got to have

some free time off. Are we giving ourselves any freedom and any relaxation? Can't keep your mind on your studies all the time. Maybe that's our trouble.

Helen: Why should I do physics and science when I'm taking home economics?

(Silence)

Jim: Has anybody told their parents about their academic probation?

Mike: When they get our marks, we won't have to tell them anything.

Frank: How long is it before marks come out?

Several voices: At least a few weeks from now.

Frank: Maybe we'll have time to pull up our marks.

Therapist: Some of you are hoping things will be better.

The two interruptions of the therapist are significant. Since the members (in this case students referred for being on academic probation) express a wish to get to know each other, the therapist responds by introducing his recorder, rather than himself, since he has already introduced himself in the beginning of the first session. He is careful to introduce the recorder by his last name, signifying to the group that by so doing he has placed the recorder with the therapist and not as a group member. The major communication of the therapist, however, is to say to the group, "I agree it is quite proper that we get to know one another." The second interruption signifies the therapist's communication, "I hear both your distress and your wish for relief."

The therapist furthers the associative process. Group action occurs rapidly and often in a way that resembles the process of free association in traditional psychoanalysis. One patient mentions an occurrence relevant to his feelings. This in turn stimulates another to respond with information relevant to himself, a third replies with a pertinent memory, a fourth makes some wandering-off gesture, and so on through the group. Even the silent members seem to resonate with what is happening, and close attention to their facial expressions and other nonverbal communication makes it clear that they also are participants. (This spread of behavior from one person to another or to a whole group is an example of what Redl calls the phenomenon of contagion.) During the occurrence of contagion, the therapist offers support through his permissive presence, his occasional supportive comments, and by encouraging nonverbal communications. Supportive comments include fragments such as, "Tell us more," "Uh huh," "What else." The major nonverbal communication involves affirmative head-shaking, and of course, a combination of all three operations is not unusual.

Notice the spread of contagion in the following excerpt from a group of college students:

> Allan: I was talking to a senior friend of mine the other day. She suggested that I change my attitude.
> Bill: That's easier said than done.
> Allan: Somehow talking about it makes me feel much better. I'm sharing it with others.
> Margo. When we ride out on the same bus in January we'll feel better too.
> Henry: Somehow I wish you wouldn't say that tonight. Let's see if we can resolve why we are all here.
> John: We're here because we're not all there.
> Allan: Maybe this is personal, but I feel I'm here to share my problems.
> Henry: Share the mess?
> Allan: I feel less tense about it now. Last Thursday I felt less tense in the math class.
> Bill: I went to my senior advisor for three weeks. I felt better seeing him than coming here.
> Therapist: Some group members are feeling less tense then.
> John: That's not my problem. I go to the library and fall asleep. I feel less tense there.

The first feature of the recording is that the material is somewhat unrelated. Patients are generally not responding to each other. No one has directly taken up Allan's opening statement that a friend suggested that he change his attitude. Nevertheless, the process of contagion is at work. The associative bond that brings the material together is the question of whether to trust the group enough to ask for help through personal sharing or to continue to express disappointment in the therapist for not offering some magical solution to their problem. The therapist maintained silence throughout most of this interchange, while giving nonverbal encouragement. His one comment served to heighten the conflict in the group, although it was intended merely to offer support in the way that has been previously described.

The therapist must communicate in such a way that the patients feel free to experience a retelling, refeeling, and reliving of emotionally-charged experiences. This retelling and reliving requires that the patient be able to express such internal material without feeling restrained by the judgment of the therapist. Here it is especially important for the therapist not to communicate parental prohibitions. Limits have previously been set by the group therapist in his initial talk with the group members. The therapist now has an additional task, namely, to emphasize a permissive atmosphere. He should achieve this both through verbal communication and through his accepting attitudes towards the group members.

In the following dialogue, Dorothy is torn between her present rootlessness, her still unresolved dependence on her parents, and her wish to find some warm, stable relationships in the present:

Dorothy: I almost thought of not seeing you again at all. I'd write, it's true, but I'm just really tired of this leaving people, you know, people I love and am close to, and then I see them later, and it's different, and I see them for an hour, it hurts.

Anna: It does.

Dorothy: I'm tired of it. I want to stay somewhere. I'm tired going through the difficulty of making friends all over again; last time let's see what I did, gave a party, why, well you're not fitting in and you don't know quite why, you know nobody will ever tell you, so you kind of feel yourself around and you get in the "in group" I guess, and then there's someone else trying to get in and you say now how can you know those guys will fit in?

Anna: Yuh, well Dorothy, it's not the same. It's for me, you know when I see someone that I haven't, you know that I've been very close with again, the old feeling just isn't there and uh, somehow it doesn't bother me like that, that old feeling isn't there, it bothers you. Maybe it does but what do you feel like, what do you want when you see someone and you feel uncomfortable for a second, what does it stir up in you?

Dorothy: The thing I always react against is that when you haven't; I think particularly of one girl out in California. I haven't seen her in four years, and so I call her, I think it's going from such a level of intensity to just barrenness almost, I don't know maybe it shouldn't have to be that way. I saw two kids from school last weekend, they came over from Boston, and you go through a strain because you haven't seen each other for years, and then so you talk about the good old times for two hours and there's no future direction from it, it's all past-oriented and it's all, gee, weren't they great times nostalgia. It's a bunch of crap! I want them now.

Anna: You mean the old relationship is gone.

Dorothy: The remnants are there, but that doesn't mean anything now, I mean I don't live in the past.

Val: And there's such a tendency with all old friends to just talk about what happened.

Dorothy: Yuh, you saw "Mary Poppins" and "Those Were the Days My Friends."

Val: Yuh, I loved it.

Dorothy: Yuh, it rings a bell.

Anna: But whenever you finish talking about the past there's nothing else to talk about.

Val: Well, you've got to separate, it's like a brief thing.

Dorothy is finally able to say with great feeling that living in the past is crap; I want my relationship in the present. Catharsis helps the patient to decently bury in the past that which belongs in the past while the patient becomes free to face the present.

While catharsis creates relief it also leads to dependency on the group members and specifically on the therapist. This dependency must be recognized and accepted or the patient may become overwhelmed with the anxiety aroused by his ventilation of feelings and his reliving experience through the retelling of past exprinces. Support then is, as defined by Alexander and French (1946), a sustaining of the individual through a period of temporary dependency. This support should come as much as possible from the group members. In the previous excerpt, Dorothy can be seen in a struggle to give up past relationships. Val finally comes through with the supporting statement when he says, "Well, you've got to separate, it's like a brief thing." The success of this statement which strongly accepts Dorothy's struggle leaves no need for the therapist to be actively supportive. The work has been done for him. This, however, is not always the case, and frequently the therapist must provide support for the group member. It is necessary to issue a caveat at this point, for a too active therapist in this regard can supply too much support and leave the patient in a state of regressed dependency, while a too passive therapist can supply too little support and leave the patient with feelings of resentment over self-exposure and abandonment. The second error is frequently made by the neophyte group leader. Two other considerations must be presented in any discussion of the use of supporting comments. These are the therapist's use of timing and the nature of the supporting statement. Timing requires that the supporting comment is made at the correct moment. The nature of the supporting statement requires that the therapist say what the patient needs to hear, that is, that the therapist's statement conveys his support in simple, straightforward terms that communicate his acceptance directly to the patient. Experience with beginning therapists requires underscoring this second point. All too frequently the academically educated therapist uses language in a decorative rather than in a communicative manner, to denote his education status much as the officer uses his insignia of rank.

Timing should be prompt and the content of the support statement should communicate acceptance without singling the patient out in any way that interrupts the flow of associations. For example:

> Don: I would have walked out at that point.
> Richard: Well, I would have been more angry.
> Don: I guess I'm saying you don't have to be as angry as you were last week.
> Richard: I would like to know why it was done. I know why I was angry because it was a surprise to me and I did not agree with the idea, and I did not get to have my say and it was my fault that I didn't get to have my say, so I was angry.

An arbitrary decision is disagreeable, I get angry. I think you can help me with that, you can tell me the reason.

Therapist: The group saw this decision as arbitrary; they haven't said so before.

Richard: It wasn't arbitrary; we weren't consulted.

Bill: It wasn't agreed on by all in a body, is that what you mean? A decision just given without warning, authoritatively rather than haphazardly.

When the therapist picks up the term *arbitrary* from Richard's long statement, he is responding *promptly* to Richard's questioning why the group was not included in the previously mentioned decision. The promptness communicates to Richard that both his question and his annoyance are accepted by the therapist and that he and the group may continue to express themselves about this problem. While Richard is not totally convinced and draws back a little from his own words, he does further develop his resentment, sharpening it to say, "We weren't consulted." Bill accepts the support and comes forward with his definition of the arbitrary behavior of the therapist.

Several techniques serve the purpose of moving patients toward a better understanding of their communication in the group and the contribution their personal dynamics are making to the communication process. These are clarification, reflection of feeling, and interpretation. Clarification is commonly understood to mean the therapist's clarification for the patients of the meaning of whatever it is that the individual patient or the group is communicating. It can also be used as a means by which the therapist can learn whether he really understands that communication is occurring in the group. In its first and most common use, clarification seems to say to the group members, "I understand that you are saying this, and I am, therefore, prepared for you to further develop this train of thought. In effect, your thinking is clear to me." A successful clarification is a testable hypothesis, and, if correct, is followed by a further development of the theme that the patients are pursuing. If incorrect, the patients may repeat the communication in another way, hoping to be understood; or they may present evidence to the therapist that he does not understand what has transpired. The use of clarification as a hypothesis to be checked against the patient's responses is shown in this selection from a session of a group of students. In the previous session, five of the thirteen members were absent. The present session deals with this sense of loss:

John: I don't think I am as angry as Diane.

Henry: Maybe that's good. She is the only one that's truthful.

Joe: Why was everyone laughing so much today?

Bill: I think the laughter was due to extreme discomfort.

Margo: I don't think so. I think it was just the opposite.

Henry: Is it scapegoating?

Joe: I don't know.

Frank: The feeling is that the whole family is here today, whereas there were five that were absent last week.

Therapist: The group is pleased that most of the members are back again. Is it then a positive feeling that the group has found it difficult to admit to today?

Joe: I wasn't here last week. It's good to be back.

Lloyd: It's good to have you . . . and you . . . and you.

Art: Last week I felt that I was intruding in the group. I didn't feel I was a member.

Jim: Perhaps you are feeling for the first time how it is.

Art: Well, at least I don't have to feel the tribulations of being an orphan this week.

Jim: I was really saying how we missed you and trying to be nice, really.

Margo is the first group member to sense that the feeling is one of pleasure rather than anger in the absent member's return. Frank responds even more positively by noting that the *family* is all together again. The therapist clarifies by stressing that the group is expressing a positive feeling. The hypothesis is validated by the subsequent group conversation. Joe is only now free to realize and share his feeling that it is good to be back, and Art's recognition that now for the first time he really feels like a group member is also expressed.

Sometimes clarification can be used in the sense of asking the group members if they are responding with a specific feeling or thought. The therapist usually phrases this type of a response as a question, and he only refers a clarification question to the group when he is in doubt about the ongoing communication. He might say, "It seems to me that the group is feeling a certain way," and wait for a direct reply which would either validate his question or clarify the nature and direction of the group's communication.

The role of the therapist in reflection requires deeply sympathetic listening and understanding. He must be both sensitive and perceptive enough to recognize the feelings and behaviors expressed in the group, and he must also have the facility to translate them into clear, verbal communications. Reflection consists of bringing to the surface and expressing in words those feelings and behaviors that lie behind the patient's words. The novice group therapist, even if he has some experience with reflection in the individual interview, will find that a reflection of a group feeling requires very sensitive listening to interactions between several individuals. He must still keep in mind the basic rule for reflection, namely, that a reflection that is unaccepted does not truly reflect what is happening or being felt at that moment in the group. Should this happen, it is not a reflection, and either reflects counter-transference fantasies of the therapist or is probably an interpretation couched in the language of a reflection.

Since the focus on patient interaction is of special concern in group psychotherapy, patients may be familiar with their self-images but show little understanding of how they are affecting others and are unaware of the effect others have on them. This includes patients' interactions with other group members and at times with the therapist. The therapist should be aware of these interactions and at times make them manifest to the patient and to the group.

In the next situation, for example, the anger is directed toward the therapist, but the group needs to know that he is both sensitive to this anger and that through recognizing it he is giving the group permission to experience it in a constructive manner. The therapist, therefore, reflects the feelings of the group.

> Martin: Why is the counselor saying "the group this" and "the group that?" If he would talk to us personally, maybe it would be better.
> Frank: Why don't you see him after this session, personally?
> Diane: That's a good idea.
> Bill: Everyone can't do it. There are only two counselors in the school.
> Martin: All we are doing is talking about who's missing.
> Lloyd: Why were you absent? Because you feel no one cares?
> Therapist: There does seem a group feeling of anger.
> Frank: At least she has admitted it.
> Marie: I don't think I'm as angry as Diane.

The therapist's reflections have permitted the group members to experience both an increased certainty of what they feel and also have freed them both to express the feeling directly and to begin to look at its consequences.

The process of interpretation has as its major goal clarifying for the patients the cause-and-effect relationship between present behaviors and past experiences. The therapist is able to do this because as a more objective observer he does not have to defend himself against the pain of understanding these cause-and-effect sequences and because he is able to translate the patient's associations into a working body of knowledge and experience that makes meaningful the patient's associations and behaviors. There are two major cautions the therapist must observe in making interpretations: he must respect the anxiety the patient feels about the understanding he is trying to ward off, and he must see that the interpretation is carefully limited to what the patient feels willing to understand and accept. The use of words like "most people," "some people," or "this could apply to you" allows patients to deny the interpretation if it is either too painful or possibly incorrect.

An additional caution states that the therapist must be

careful to use interpretation sparingly, for interpretation moves the relationship from the patient's frame of reference to the therapist's, and the therapist who enjoys taking the center of the stage can readily reduce the patient to an audience.

The following session illustrates the therapist taking the lead by moving from the here-and-now associations that are part of the patient's frame of reference to an interpretation which attempts to clarify the cause-and-effect relations concerning the patient's dissatisfaction with Dr. D., the cotherapist.

> Robert: I like it better when Dr. D. responds personally, whether it's to me as a person in a discussion we are having or something that's going on in the group.
> Steve: Yes, I agree.
> George: Yes, I wish we could have been closer.
> Dr. W.: Has Dr. D. not always been a good mother?
> Steve: What's that!
> Dr. D.: Steve's contemplating.
> Steve: She's a teacher rather than a mother. I thought that's what I heard you saying.

In this case, the association between Dr. D. and mother is too difficult for Steve to accept. Its impact, however, was not lost on the group, for in the next session Belle spent most of the hour discussing under great emotional strain her own relationship to her parents.

Although the objective of interpretation is the uncovering of a cause-and-effect relationship for the patient or patients in the group, its expression can be couched in many forms. These can be ordered on a continuum from tentative to direct. The most tentative expression has the value of communicating to the patients both that they have the options of refusing the statement and that the therapist wishes to advance the statement as a possibility to be checked out by the group. An explanation is probably the most tentative form of interpretation. The explanation is a descriptive statement and should be neutral in tone. For example, the therapist might say, "In being quiet, here in the group, you are behaving much as you did at home with your family."

Somewhat less tentative than explanation is suggestion.

Suggestion, a mild form of advice, does not demand compliance if the patients reject it. Indeed, suggestion should have the effect of stimulating the group members to think about that suggestion as a possible reason that certain motives and behaviors go together. The therapist addresses a group member, "That sounds psychological, possibly your backache is related to your difficulty in carrying Chemistry 112." The question, a third means of advancing interpretation, can be used to elicit motives. When it is used this way the approach is no longer tentative and the therapist is expecting the group or group member to follow along his line of thinking. When the therapist says, "Tell me more about that," he is definitely taking the lead and is preparing the patient and the group to focus on a specific area. The clearest and most direct form of interpretation is an explanation of a motive, which involves relating a patient's need to his present behavior. Explanation of a motive should be used sparingly, and only when the therapist feels the patient is prepared.

The principal dynamic operating in the therapy group can best be identified as group movement. Group movement can be recognized by a sudden expression of awareness by group members of what is occurring in the group at a specific moment. This awareness, even if verbalized by a single patient, is accepted by other group members who follow with a chain of associations that both reflect the awareness and prepare them to move to communicate a new theme. Prior to the sudden shift that signals movement, the group struggles to develop a theme that will communicate both to its members and to the therapist the conflict with which the group is working.

The theme takes its name from the observation made by a number of writers in this field that apparently unrelated remarks of several patients may reflect a common concern in the group. These common concerns can be tied together and can be said to represent the theme of a given session. Themes are, therefore, abstractions of the significant relationships in the group therapy session between patients and between patients and therapists. Themes can be identified from the topics, attitudes, and feelings expressed by the patients in the group therapy session. A single major theme seems to predominate in each therapy session.

Winder and Hersko (1958) have identified nine themes occurring in a group that met weekly for seventy-seven sessions. These were: (1) hostility toward authority figure; (2) hostility toward peers; (3) warmth toward authority figure; (4) warmth toward peers; (5) expression of need for help; (6) fear of losing self-control; (7) responsibility for self and others; (8) jealousy; (9) recognition of dependency. A theme may appear only once or in sequence. If it appears in sequence, the theme will have a "run," and a run may last two or more sessions. In the event that the theme is not recognized and dealt with by the therapist and the group, it may be dropped temporarily and reappear at a later session.

Movement may be recognized not only by the sudden open awareness in group conversation of the theme that has been struggling for expression but also by the emergence of a minor theme appearing in the same therapy hour. The presence of a minor theme about which the group members' talk begins to cluster, signals to everyone present that the group wishes to move on to another concern.

Why, perhaps reader asks at this point, does not the theme appear readily to both therapist and patient alike almost as soon as it is articulated? Movement is retarded and the meaning of the theme is obscured by patient resistance in dealing with the painful material that would emerge and be communicated if only they could speak directly of their concerns. The therapist must, therefore, deal in ways mentioned in the preceding section, with the resistances of the group member before both he and the group can be aware of, and deal with, the themes themselves.

Earlier in this chapter, Erikson's (1959) theory of ego development was outlined as a working theory of personality that can be of great help to the group therapist. It was pointed out that the individual strives for a sense of trust in others, an autonomy that gives him a sense of self-determination, an initiative that permits him to select goals and persevere, and finally an identity that will integrate the fragments of his experience into a totality.

Resistances can, therefore, be seen as motivated by the anxiety that serves as a warning signal, alerting the individual to painful thoughts and feelings, or ego dystonic actions may emerge into consciousness. Resistances also can be seen as serving the function of continuing those aspects of the nuclear conflicts of childhood that have become embedded in the patient's characteristic behaviors; namely, those that perpetuate in the individual a sense of mistrust, doubt, and guilt. Dangers to these characteristic ways of organizing perception, thought, feeling, and action are signaled to the individual by anxiety—by a subjective experiencing of tension through irritability, depression, or through physiological concomitants of autonomic instability. Indications include cerebral sweating (wet palms), queasy stomach, hyperventilation, vasomotor instability (cold hands), and many others. Some individuals experience anxiety directly in this fashion; other move immediately into protective operations. For most individuals, both some experience of anxiety and the taking over of protection operations occurs. These attempts at protection permit the continuance in the individual of characteristic attitudes of mistrust, self-doubt, and guilt.

Early in group therapy the patients are faced with the requirement of experiencing a sense of trust both for their fellow members and for the therapist. Resistance to this development usually follows along the lines of denial, silence, and anger.

Denial signifies an unwillingness to acknowledge one's behavior and its implications. This is an infantile attitude by which the patients simply "will away" that which they refuse to face, usually covering an intense anxiety which they hope will go away because they insist it is not there. In early group sessions denial takes the form of patients' insisting that their problems are not of interest to anyone; they see no sense in talking about their problems in front of others.

In interaction between the patient and the therapist, denial generally takes the form of patient behavior that demands some magical relief through actions on the part of the therapist that will bypass any necessity for establishing a sense of trust with him. Denial is usually followed by silence. While silence may resist therapeutic movement in several ways, in the initial sessions, it is a deliberate holding back of self, usually for punishing the therapist and occasionally the other group members. In this form of resistance, patients refuse to share themselves. Suspicious of the therapist who demands a sense of trust and fearful of the reaction of other group members, they sit quietly and docile. As patients are further importuned to trust, a third resistance emerges, anger. The patients at this point are beginning to feel a loss of their defensive posture. Hostilities then rise quickly to the surface. If the patients attack and strike a hard blow, they may drive their tormentor away. The therapist must be careful at this point to confront the patients with the fact that he has been demanding the development of natural trust and open communication between group members. If he does this, he will become the focus of attack; if, however, he neglects this confrontation, the patients may displace their anger on to one of their own number. This action is generally termed scapegoating. The scapegoat is usually a patient who shows little tolerance for the conflict in the group. He is for this reason less able than the others to contribute to the specific form of resistance, either denial or silence, that the group is currently using. He is the one, in effect, who communicates "let's give this up, I can't stand it a minute longer." The therapist's role in this case is always to interpret this displacement of anger that the group has preferred to direct against one of their members. His interpretation refocuses the anger around the original resistance and allows the group to proceed toward the development of trust.

A significant movement toward trust between group members and the therapist activates the group members into the position of taking responsibility for reporting their own personal histories through their individual styles of communication. These communications may range from there-and-then experiences dealing with either the near or distant past, fantasy productions (mainly dreams), and here-and-now confrontations with fellow patients and the therapist. To speak openly and honestly both about one's self and to others involves a freedom to make decisions without a grave sense of self-doubt or an overwhelming sense of shame in front of others. Both self-doubt and shame engender their own resistances, and even a group that has developed an initial sense of trust seems still to need these resistances before they can achieve the autonomy that permits forthright expression both to self and others.

Various kinds of escape mechanisms are put in operation by patients who are struggling with autonomy. Indeed, Fromm (1941) has made the theme "Escape from Freedom" a central characteristic of the behavior of modern man. Escape can take the form of silence. Silence used in this way is an escape from the discomfort of conflict. Silence becomes an escape from self-disclosure by the simple expedient of refusing to speak. But refusal to speak within the group situation is not a simple expedient and usually leads the patients into a struggle with their own ambivalence. On the one hand, they wish to remain silent and hold on to their thoughts and feelings; on the other hand, they wish to let go and share these thoughts and emotions with the others. Should the therapist communicate directly or indirectly that the patients are compelled to speak, they feel exploited and robbed of their decision-making power. They then become both resentful of the external pressure manifested by the therapist and guilty over the pressure within themselves to keep things going. At this point, the beginning therapist frequently finds himself engaged in a battle of wills with the patients who are determined to wait him out. Proper clarification of the difficulty the group members are facing, plus encouraging them to explore the reasons for their silence, is usually effective in these circumstances.

Absenteeism also can be used as an escape. Absenteeism can frustrate even the most experienced therapist, for if the patient is missing, the meaning of his resistance cannot be worked upon (since absenteeism is more likely to occur when the group is working on autonomy than at any other time). The other group members when confronted with the meaning of this form of resistance will frequently take the responsibility to persuade the absent member to return to the group. (It should be noted that absence may occur with an inexperienced therapist in the initial group meetings, usually during a crisis of trust and frequently becoming a permanent dropping out with the therapist unable to control the outcome.) Absence can frequently have a dual purpose, for the patient may be also asking how much his contribution has been valued by the others. "Have I been missed?" can mean how much does the group value one's contribution; furthermore, knowledge of one's importance to the group can be a valuable antidote to self-doubt. Lateness is usually a variation on the theme of absence, but the escape is only an implied threat, held over the group and the therapist if the patient's freedom of expression is either unappreciated or likely to be punished. Patients frequently make excuses for both absence and tardiness. Obviously, sometimes the excuses are legitimate: buses do not run, trains are late, patients are ill. The therapist should be guided by the group communications at the time. If the group is in a stage of resistance against growth in autonomy, the patient's act of being late or absent is probably part of that resistance and the excuses serve as rationalizations.

Patients use rationalization and projection frequently when they are struggling to assert and experience their autonomy. Projection is the process through which an unacceptable internal tendency is unrealistically attributed to another. Its process of development in the psychotherapy group usually begins when a member of the group blames or berates others in his world for what is actually his own refusal to assume responsibility for his behavior. Objects of blame usually are teachers, bosses, parents, or spouses, and the projection usually serves to cover up the unacceptable passivity and dependency that the patients feel towards these figures. The therapist's acceptance of such expressions of blame leads to the contagion of feeling among the group members that they can displace blame directly upon him. The therapist must then proceed to help the group to recognize their wish to be passive and dependent in his presence and to see that the recognition of their wishes frees them to act autonomously.

Rationalization serves also to defend the patients against passive and dependent wishes. Unlike projection, this form of resistance cloaks one's inability to act with false, but seemingly relevant, reasons. "I can't help it," becomes a paradigm for the basic statement of rationalization, with variations of the sentence beginning after the word "because." Other patients become very adept at seeing the irrelevance of the because clause, and they become skilled at questioning the motives utilized by the inveterate rationalizer.

Closely related to the use of projection is the phobic quality of the group when concerned with the problems of autonomy. This phobic quality, which usually involves an unreasonable fear of attack, can be detected by the over-talkativeness of group members. One or two group members for whom this is an accustomed mode of behavior under stress may lead the way, but the group as a whole seems to divide between those with great need to speak and those

who would encourage them as if they were providing great amuse-
ment or great wisdom or both. Such talkativeness delays the attack
that the patients expect. The underlying use of projection is present,
both in viewing the therapist as an offensive, punitive figure, and
in the content of the talk. This content is replete with injustices
unfairly heaped upon individual group members resulting from un-
feeling authority figures in their daily lives.

Finally, group members, in an effort to avoid confronting
passive and dependent wishes that hobble their efforts toward autonomy, become frustrated and rebellious. They attack the therapy
openly: "What's the good of this?" They disparage the value of
the experience: "It isn't helping me!" They attack the therapist:
"You haven't helped me at all!" The beginning practitioner may
feel threatened by such an attack. His confidence may be shaken in
therapy as a curative approach to human problems, or in his ability
to conduct the process, or in himself as a sensitive and understanding human being. It is important for him to recall that both his
knowledge of personality dynamics and of the theory of group
psychotherapy predict this form of resistance and require him to
confront the patients with the motivations for their behavior.

Resistances to the development of initiative are resistances
that bar one from setting goals and pursuing them effectively.
Primary among these resistances is depression. Patients feel low
and dejected. They can give no reason for this sense of gloom. A
young man, for example, is unsure of whether he wishes to continue
in college. He argues with his father. He is enraged that his father
demands that he "grow up." He feels a threat to his developing
masculinity, a gnawing questioning of his personal adequacy. The
expression of these feelings toward his father could destroy a continuing need for his father's protection, and in addition he has
fantasies of strong parental retaliation if he were to dare to express
hostility. His feelings, therefore, are discharged in depression rather
than in anger. Melancholy, while it leaves one unable to move in
any direction, is, nevertheless, the more acceptable mood.

A group member experiencing this kind of depression will
easily become a focus of group concern. Should the group offer the
member brief sympathetic or common sense advice and then pass
on to other topics, the group is telling him that they are not yet

ready to work on the problems of developing initiative. If, however, the depression spreads to the group and the members respond with feeling, action, and content that is indicative of sadness and gloom, then the group is prepared to deal with this form of resistance.

The conversion in the group of feelings of sadness into feelings of anger is generally accompanied by the phenomenon of displacement. The hostile feelings of group members are displaced from the person or persons in the patient's past who first caused him to feel this way. These displacements tend to fall first on such real authority figures as foremen, supervisors, principals, and deans, then on to a group member who demonstrates authoritarian attitudes, and finally, upon the therapist. At this point, the therapist becomes the embodiment of the powerful parental figure, an object of fantasy, who the group believes will not permit them to grow.

The decision to leave treatment may be a sign that a group member has adequately worked through his problems. A patient who mentions this desire for the purpose of sharing this possibility with his group and therapist should expect some consensual validation of his belief that he has made substantial progress. Should such a decision come early in the group's life and be accompanied by a seemingly convincing citing of improvements in the patient's behavior, then the patient is using the decision to serve as a resistance to further treatment. Comments that indicate a "flight into health" are common. "I never felt better, no more depression, no more worries," or, "My marks have improved, I think I'll take off, after all, I have to be able to solve my own problems," are typical. These optimistic statements contain an element of truth, for the patient must demonstrate to himself, to the group, and to the therapist that he is leaving only because he has successfully completed the program of treatment. Other patients will sense that the patient's statements are only partially true, for basically, his flight into health is defensive and temporary; behind it lies his refusal to come to terms with his passive and dependent wishes and to struggle for a sense of personal initiative. The other patients will look to see if the therapist is willing to struggle with this group member to help him through the difficulties of his conflict around initiative and guilt, or whether the group member is fearful of the struggle and will accept a "token cure." If the therapist shows his commitment to work through the conflict from which the patient is escaping, the other group members will rally around the frightened individual whose defensive wish is to leave and they will offer him clarification and interpretation of his present behavior. Should the arguments of the group members fail to make any impact on his decision to remain, the group members will, in spite of their lack of success in persuading him, let him know that he is still an integral part of their group and that there is a place for him should he wish to return.

The quest for identity is defined by Erikson (1962, p. 6) as "the search for something and somebody to be true to." The group, with its obvious reliance upon peer interaction and with a therapist upon whom it is all too easy to transfer parental images, presents a structure psychologically similar to that experienced by most individuals during their teen-age years. This structure provides patients in the sixteen-to-twenty-year range a chance to work on problems of identity formation. Adult patients can, within this structure, readily regress and recreate the attitudes and feelings attendant upon their previous identity crises. The group, then, provides the opportunity for both age levels to work upon their incomplete commitment to future goals which can develop only through one's belief in another human being. Resistances to commitment then must take the form of intense questioning of the therapist, one's peers, and outside associates. To give one's fidelity to another youth demands that the other pass tests of authenticity and genuineness of feeling. This questioning of individuals and ideologies takes the form outside the therapy group of significant encounters with others. These encounters that parents, authorities, and friends experience with individuals seeking a way out of an identity crisis can lead to severe estrangement between the patient and those whom he hopes will help him. Patients bring to the group examples of inauthenticity, hypocrisy, and emotional and intellectual shallowness derived from their encounters with significant people in their environments. There is a danger here that the beginning therapist will see these attacks on theology, questioning of morality, and diatribes against the establishment as social conversation that belongs outside the group. Should he view such subject matter in this manner and state that the group's values and beliefs are no proper subject for the group since this does not deal with individual problems, the therapist will be encouraging acting out as the only means of communication with him. Unfortunately, the real world will not view the patient's acting out as a therapeutic communication, albeit somewhat hysterical; rather, the police, the dean, or the boss will set consequences in motion that will result in arrest, failure, or dismissal.

It is incumbent upon the therapist to recognize that the patients are attempting to determine his commitment to them as patients. Is he an authentic helper? Is he a caring person? Are his feelings toward them genuine? The therapist's success in understanding the importance of these questions and his ability to communicate his own authenticity will prepare the way for the patients to seek others in the real world who will be suitable objects of identification. Should the therapist fail to do so, he will have to deal with the depression and withdrawal that characterize career inhibition, the interpersonal problems that characterize sexual confusion, and the resulting acting out that leads to society's confirmation of the individual as a failure.

Up to this point, we have discussed a theoretical model of group psychotherapy and a number of treatment techniques that follow from this model. We have not discussed specific goals for a group since these follow from the nature of the group with which the therapist is working. For example: a group of college students needs to work through the problems attendant upon an identity crisis; a group of parents who have placed their children in a residential treatment center may have to work through the guilt that accompanies abandonment of a child and the temporary abrogation of their parental role. Goals, therefore, depend upon the conflict or conflicts that are mobilized in the group members by the nature of the developmental stresses they are facing. In the case of the theoretical model supplied by Erikson, one or more conflicts related to one or more of his developmental levels are mobilized by the stress of life and cause the members to seek help.

A theoretical model of group therapy, a technique of treatment, and a goal for the patients are not enough for the therapist to feel that he has exhausted all his opportunities to make a contribution to human welfare. He must now ask what specific variables operating within the context of the therapy group have contributed to improvement or lack of improvement in the patient's behavior. When the therapist asks this question, he shifts from his role as therapist and assumes the role of investigator. Once he has asked why certain phenomena have occurred, wishing to seek a satisfactory explanation, he must seek a new model, the model of science.

Science may be defined as any body of organized knowledge which has been obtained by using the method of relevant, systematic observation. There are many ways of obtaining knowledge, and what distinguishes scientific from nonscientific knowledge is the approach followed in obtaining the results. The distinguishing characteristic of the scientific approach or method is the use of relevant, systematic observation. The making of observations then provides the data used in answering the question under investigation. However, an immediate complexity which appears in making observations about human behavior takes the form of the need to discriminate between behavior that is directly observable and that behavior whose attributes and processes must be inferred. For example, if the patient colors, raises his voice, clenches his fist, and says to the therapist, "You are a quack," the therapist may observe that the patient is exhibiting angry behavior. The therapist may conclude that the patient is projecting his hostility and displacing it into his person. This conclusion deals with an aspect of the patient's behavior that has not been observed directly in the patient: it is an inference made from his behavior. It will be seen later that frequently the questions asked about what is occurring within a therapy group require the investigator to make inferences from observations if he is to obtain an answer to those questions.

Two basic concepts necessary for the understanding of research in human behavior are those of independent and dependent variables. The independent variable refers to the question being asked by the investigator. The question most frequently asked by group therapists is: does group therapy result in patient improvement? Since World War II this question has been the subject of much research. Bednar (1970), in a review of research on group psychotherapy from the two decades, 1945 through 1965, reports that 60 percent of the studies reported have asked this question, therefore using group therapy as the independent variable. Recent investigators have realized that the group therapy process itself is subject to a wide range of definitions and that if it is to be a useful tool in communication to others in the field, it should be specified according to four major dimensions. These are: definition of the theoretical model used by the therapist, the treatment techniques that have been applied, the specific goals that have been defined for the group under consideration, and the therapeutic orientation of the therapist. Bednar further reports that there has been a recent increasing willingness to isolate and study specific variables that may contribute to the patient's improvement. For example, a specific question that has been raised is, how does the composition of the group contribute to patient improvement? Once raised, the question can be identified as the independent variable and varied through the development of a research design that will permit the setting up of groups of different compositions of patients. It then becomes possible to observe the effects of differing group compositions on behavior changes occurring in the patient.

Other specific independent variables that have been isolated for study include the nature of the group therapist, the method of treatment based upon a given theoretical model, and the content areas discussed by the group. Some examples of studies that have made a contribution through identifying specific variables are treated in Truax's study on the effects of empathy, warmth, genuineness, interpersonal concreteness, and depth of self-exploration (1961). Further examples are: the investigation by Kapp and others of the relationship between group unity and personal involvement (1964), Sechrest and Barger's research into meaningful verbal participation (1961), and Yalom and Rand's investigation of group popularity and group cohesion (1966).

The dependent variable refers to the aspect of human behavior being studied by means of observing its behavioral manifestations. It has already been mentioned that these behavioral changes can sometimes be observed directly and sometimes must be inferred from direct observation. Much research dealing with group therapy and either its effect or the effect of certain processes occurring during the therapy have made use of direct observation as the criteria of patient improvement. Some of these directly observable behavior criteria were: (1) academic grades have been a popular criterion when dealing with school populations; (2) the amount of time spent out of the hospital after discharge, the rate of return to the hospital, and the frequency of disturbances on the ward caused by the patient have proved to be easily observable criteria of success with the hospitalized neuropsychiatric population; (3) violation of the rules of conduct after therapy have been easily observable indices of success or failure of treatment with populations diagnosed as delinquent. It should be noted that while this list provides an illustration rather than a totality of such criteria, most research on the effects of treatment on patient behavior include at least one of these criterion variables.

However sometimes when the researcher poses questions that cannot be answered by direct observation, it becomes necessary for him to make use of instruments that give some satisfactory measure of the inferred behavioral characteristics. Suppose the researcher should ask about the effect of group therapy on the patient's self perception or on his level of intellectual functioning. These attributes of behavior are generally considered to be within the individual and not accessible to direct observation. Fortunately, researchers now have a range of instruments that can be applied to measure change in the dependent variable that reflects differences within individuals when these differences are not directly observable. The most sophisticated of these instruments are taken from the field of psychometrics. Tests of intellectual function with high coefficients of reliability and validity are readily available. The Wechsler Bellevue Intelligence Scale is a favorite of clinical workers.

Dependent variables that reflect changes in attitudes towards self or others can be measured by use of the semantic differential, the "Q" sort behavioral rating scales, and attitude check lists. While the latter two instruments are statistically less refined than the former, they have been sufficiently developed to offer a satisfactory level of objectivity in measurement. There is some controversy in the field of psychological measurement over projective techniques as valid measures of inferred personality traits. We believe, however, that the Rorschach and Thematic Apperception Test will, when placed in the hands of a trained interpreter, yield very valuable data.

The outlook for immediate future research in this field can best be expressed in a quote from "The Summary of the Group

Psychotherapy Literature," where MacLennon and Levy (1969, p. 383) state, "Although there are many more reports of research on group treatment than in the past, there still remains a lack of coherence between goals, method and outcome, and a general uncertainty as to how to judge the quality of treatments or the effectiveness of therapists."

Chapter IV

≽≽≽≼≼≼

Training Groups: Theory and Practice

People come to training groups to learn, and the first task of the participants in a T-group will be learning how to learn. This means coming with some commitment to examine old ideas, attitudes, values, and behaviors and to try out new ones in a "temporary society" with the expectation that these learnings may be taken with them to a back-home environment. It is the participant's task to act, to look at his own behavior, to examine his interpersonal effectiveness, to see how other people are, and to learn how groups and organizations function. He will learn something about how to plan for change in all of these systems and how to evaluate all of these attempts.

The first task of the trainer is to arrange the early environment in such a way that these explorations can take place, that is, to help create a collaborative growth-oriented learning environment through what he or she does and says and is, something which differs from the everyday, competitive, survival-oriented environment of the participants' back home world. Ideally, the training program itself is a paradigm for the values and goals the staff bring to the laboratory along with their skills, knowledge, and experience. Thus are the metagoals of the laboratory method demonstrated *in vivo—a spirit of inquiry, collaboration, conflict resolution through rational means, and the freedom to exercise choice* are lived by the staff and shared by the participants.

Here can be tested, in relative safety, a world in which *trust, risk-taking, openness, and interdependence* are possible. Participants then have the opportunity to examine and experience this alternative model, and the option to choose it or not after the program. Is it viable? Are interpersonal and group effectiveness increased? Is this model of a helping relationship desirable? It is surely not an easy task to create such a learning environment, and yet it is, we would say, the single most essential ingredient for an effective reeducation program. Whether or not the trainer can do this is not entirely up to him, but it is, at first, primarily his responsibility.

Some common limitations are: limited time, the composition of the group, the expectations and needs of the participants, the sponsor of the laboratory and its location; and all are combined with expectations and needs of particular staff members, and the design of the laboratory. On the other hand, traditionally, the situation is helped by unique circumstances: a group of strangers who meet together in an isolated setting, away from the role-related and historical limitations placed on them back home. History for these people starts in the here-and-now, and the trainer will help to keep attention focused on data which are available to all through their experiences together. He will share his knowledge and skills as a unique member of this group and become dispensable as his special functions are taken over by the other members. In all of this, the most important contribution of the trainer is his philosophy, his belief in the metagoals of the laboratory, and his ability to demonstrate them.

There is, according to Reisel (1962), a heavy overtone of social responsibility on the trainer. There is a commitment to sharing a philosophy of collaboration with individuals who have had little experience with this model, of demonstrating that openness to feelings and risk-taking with others can be productive. He will have to work hard to avoid the all-too-easy flight into authority always open in the role if the participants are to understand the alternative help-sharing, not help-giving, model.

Given a climate of threat to self-esteem, competition, and so forth, a survival orientation is engaged and individuals become defensive and fall back on their traditional role-related behaviors. It is important to create an environment in which "survival" is not the issue; an environment in which "people's general tendency toward *optimal* exploration and variety" (Clark, 1963, p. 8) might be set in motion. It cannot be foretold exactly what will happen because, as Bradford (1964) says, the trainer does not control the process; rather, he helps the group develop adequate methods of inquiry. In the T-group it is the method of inquiry itself which gives direction and controls process. And the trainer, being better skilled in this method, is therefore able to help the others.

It is worthwhile to postpone briefly an examination of the T-group itself to further highlight the differences between the assumptions about motivation and the nature of human beings which are traditionally held by many people in the *help-giving* professions, and the very different assumptions which need to be understood by the *help-sharing* training staff if they are to offer an alternative learning/action model.

For many years, until his death, Maslow (1962, 1970) was concerned with establishing "higher ceilings for human nature" by using as a measure "what could be," that is, peak experiences, as opposed to looking at "what is" as the measure. He tells us that "human life will never be understood unless its highest aspirations are taken into account. Growth, self-actualization, the striving toward health . . . the yearning for excellence . . . must by now be accepted beyond question as a widespread and perhaps universal tendency" (Maslow, 1970, pp. xii–xiii). Although he had tried to build upon the classical psychologies of behaviorism and Freudian psychoanalysis when he first wrote *Motivation and Personality* in 1954, by the time he wrote the revised edition in 1970, he was ready to say that there is now a new *Zeitgeist*, a new general comprehensive philosophy of life. "This new 'humanistic' *Weltenschauung* seems to be a new and far more helpful, hopeful and encouraging way of conceiving any and every area of human knowledge: e.g., economics, sociology, biology, and every profession: e.g., law, politics, medicine, and all of the social institutions: e.g., the family, education, religion, etc. I have acted upon this personal conviction in revising this book, writing into the psychology presented herein the belief that it is an aspect of a much broader world view and of a comprehensive life-philosophy, which is already partly worked out, at least to the point of plausibility, and must, therefore, be taken seriously" (Maslow, 1970, p. x).

Maslow was convinced that his theory of motivation had been "quite successful in a clinical, social, and personological way, but not in a laboratory and experimental way" (Maslow, 1970, p. xii). He was encouraged by the work of McGregor (1960), who applied this theory to the industrial situation. It was useful to McGregor, who could make sense out of his data and observations, and in turn was validation for the theory as well. Maslow then looked forward to such empirical support rather than traditional experimental support. As he says, "Obviously it needs a life situation of the total human being in his social environment. This is where confirmation or disconfirmation will come from" (Maslow, 1970, xii). (The training laboratory can also act as a confirming or disconfirming place.)

McGregor, building on the work of Maslow, distinguished between the traditional management view of direction and control which he called "Theory X" and a collaborative model of management called "Theory Y." Each is based on assumptions about human nature and human behavior and lead to very different ways of setting the environment and relating to people. Theory X assumes that the average human being has an inherent dislike of work and will avoid it if he can. Because of this human characteristic dislike of work, most people must be coerced, controlled, directed, and threatened with punishment to get them to put forth adequate effort toward the achievement of organizational objectives. The average person prefers to be directed, wishes to avoid responsibility, has relatively little ambition, and wants security above all. Theory Y, on the other hand, assumes that the expenditure of physical and mental effort in work is as natural as play or rest. External control and the threat of punishment are not the only means for bringing about effort toward organizational objectives. Man will exercise self-direction and self-control in the service of objectives to which he is committed. Commitment to objectives is a function of the rewards associated with their achievement, for example, ego and self-realization. Under proper conditions, the average human being learns not only to accept but to seek responsibility. The capacity to exercise a relatively high degree of imagination, ingenuity, and creativity in the solution of organizational problems is widely, not narrowly, distributed in the population. Under the conditions of modern industrial life, the intellectual potentialities of the average human being are only partially utilized. (McGregor, 1960, abridged from chapters 3 and 4.)

Tannenbaum and Davis (1969), going beyond McGregor, want to affirm their values which they believe are compatible with relevant findings emerging in the behavioral sciences. These values are: away from a view of man as essentially bad toward a view of him as basically good; away from avoidance or negative evaluation of individuals toward confirming them as human beings; away from a view of individuals as fixed toward seeing them as being in process; away from resisting and fearing individual differences toward accepting and utilizing them; away from utilizing an individual primarily with reference to his job description toward viewing him as a whole person; away from walling off the expression of feelings toward making possible both appropriate expression and effective use; away from use of status for maintaining power and personal prestige toward use of status for organizationally relevant purposes; away from distrusting people toward trusting them; away from avoiding facing others with relevant data toward making appropriate confrontation; away from avoidance of risk-taking toward willingness to risk; away from a view of process work as being unproductive effort toward seeing it as essential to effective task accomplishment; away from a primary emphasis on competition toward a much greater emphasis on collaboration. They conclude the discussion of these values by saying: "In addition to this bias towards optimism, there has to be a recognition of the fundamental fact that we will continuously have to deal with resistance to change, including resistances within ourselves. People are not standing in line outside our doors asking to be freed up, liberated, and up-ended. Cultures are not saying: 'Change us, we can no longer cope, we are unstable.' Commitment to trying to implement these values as well as we can is not commitment to an easy, safe existence" (Tannenbaum and Davis, 1969, p. 24).

Although it is true that there are individuals whose developmental conflicts are not resolved (see Chapter Three, discussion of Erikson) and who desire therapy, it should be more clearly recognized that T-groups are not (and should not be) a substitute for therapy and that trainers should be setting learning environments for here-and-now problem-solving and transfer of learnings, not for regression and transference resolutions. It should be recognized that there *are* healthy, effectively functioning people who do not need to be controlled by "management"—as in help-giving models—but rather can be self-directed and self-controlled, and therefore can respond to help-sharing models of the laboratory method. It is unnecessary to put everything into a remedial or therapeutic frame of reference even when that model seems to provide all the answers (Gottschalk, 1971). For example, it can be said that an individual is hostile if he arrives at meetings late; if he arrives early, he is anxious; and if he arrives on time, he is compulsive. But that need not be the only frame of reference for understanding his behavior.

It is important to recognize that growth theories of motivation are not synonymous with the myth of the happy person, just as peer group does not equal play group. The difference is primarily one of viewing people as potentially proactive rather than necessarily reactive. So instead of assuming you must make an individual uncomfortable (shake him up, take away his usual coping behavior), the theory assumes that healthy individuals will seek out new situations, will take risks, will create problems, and then will engage in problem-solving behavior—not in the repetitious, self-destructive cycle of unresolved conflicts presenting themselves over and over again but in conflict-free, intentional risk-taking. Maslow (1970) reminds us, however, that the growth instincts are weak and the security and safety needs are very strong. The choice of risk over safety must be made over and over again. The environment must not stifle these growth tendencies, nor tip the balance in favor of regression over growth.

Although *what* is done in a group may not be different for different trainers, there is a difference in the *how:* the managing trainer, waiting to give to and do for the participants, changes to an ennabler who confirms their competence as participants prove and improve their interpersonal competence. In that case, we can assume that effectiveness of organizations, institutions, groups, and individuals will be increased, not decreased, as a result of training experiences. Work becomes an important and enjoyable, that is, a confirming (not happiness-producing) experience.

However, organizations will have to change, also: "Human beings who have gone through the somewhat painful reeducation to value growth will tend to find the present organizational structures not only frustrating but discouraging. We suggest that the organization of the future will also strive to enlarge the jobs" (Argyris, 1964, p. 274).

The T-group provides such an opportunity to find out "what can be," given a growth-oriented, collaborative environment. Although it is unlikely that anyone resolves all of his developmental conflicts totally, still: "Therapy and competence acquisition have similar objectives: to help individuals behave more competently. Each change activity differs from the other primarily in terms of the learning conditions that it creates, and, therefore, in terms of the different clients who can be helped by experiencing it. Competence acquisition is more relevant when the subjects are unconflicted enough so that (a) they are less survival-oriented and more competence-oriented and (b) they are able to generate for and learn from one another, because of their ability to comunicate minimally distorted, directly validatable, and minimally evaluative information in such a way that (c) they are able to trust themselves and the other group members as resources for learning" (Argyris, 1968, p. 177).

As we shall see, for a group to grow and develop it requires that there be at least some *independent* individuals, that is, individuals not conflicted about dependency and authority by being overly dependent or counterdependent and not conflicted about intimacy and interdependence by being overly personal or counterpersonal. As the group develops, these individuals will be able to move the group past their struggles with power and love, authority and intimacy—even if some of the participants are conflicted (Bennis and Shepard, 1956). (Parenthetically, we might add that if the group can move only as quickly as the most conflicted member (Whitman, 1964), then there is even more need to make the differences between therapy and T-groups clear to participants.) What the optimally desirable mix would be is a problem Harrison (1965) has been working on.

If the T-group could count on attracting only *self-actualizing* individuals, as Maslow (1970) defined them, then we could expect all of them to find this new situation a challenge rather than a threat. However, such individuals are rare. Nevertheless, even if it is a stressful situation at first for some participants, it should not be *designed* to be overwhelmingly threatening: that is, participants, it should be assumed, can mobilize problem-solving behavior, and the situation should be so arranged that it does not assume nor force regression as a necessary condition for reeducation.

One way to better understanding how this "healthy" stress can be generated is by briefly looking at the Schein and Bennis (1965) theory of how learning takes place in a T-group. It is based on Lewin's change theory and assumes a three-stage change process. At first, there is an unfreezing stage, where the participant feels a need to do something and feels safe enough in the environment to do it; then he must find some interpersonal cues or a model that leads him to try out some new behavior; he must also find some confirmation for that behavior; and then occurs a refreezing stage where the change is integrated intrapersonally and interpersonally. This progression involves increased awareness, changed attitudes, and interpersonal competence in a continuing cyclical process, which is described by Schein and Bennis (1965) as follows: (a) dilemma or disconcerting information; (b) attitude change about how to learn (acceptance of metagoals); (c) generation of new behavior which makes new information available; (d) increased awareness and/or new disconfirmation; (e) attitude change about self and others; (f) new behavior, hence new information; (g) increased awareness and/or new disconfirmation; (h) further attitude change until termination or equilibrium.

Another way to understand how experienced competence is reinvested to lead to greater self-confirmation is described by Hampden-Turner as "the cycle of human experience." His existential learning theory takes the form of a self-perpetuating cycle which, in a relatively mature stage development, would read as follows: According to (a) the quality of an individual's cognition, (b) the clarity of his identity, and (c) the extent of his self-esteem, (d) all three of which he orders into a purposeful synthesis of his experienced and anticipated competence, (e) the subject invests with a degree of autonomy in his human environment by (f) periodically "letting go" and risking a portion of his experienced competence. He will thus (g) try to "bridge the distance" between himself and the Other and (h) seek self-confirmation through the impact of his invested competence upon the Other. (i) According to the enhancement (or reduction) experienced by the Other, the latter will reinvest (or avoid) in a manner which moves toward synergy (or conflict). (j) The investor will attempt to integrate the feedback from this exchange into a mental map whose breadth and complexity are a measure of investing success. And according to (a), (b), and (c) at that time, the cycle continues (1966, 367–368).

Following White (1959), Argyris (1965) offers a well-articulated position about the importance of interpersonal competence and how this is developed. He arbitrarily distinguishes interpersonal competence from intellectual cognitive competence, "for analytical convenience," so that he can pursue the question of what happens to the intellectual competence given varying amounts of interpersonal competence. Central to his position is the interdependence and interresponsibility of the individual and the group. There is a need for freedom with responsibility; improved interpersonal competence should mean also improved group and/or organizational effectiveness. But that does not grow out of freedom from responsibility nor repression of the individual through fear for survival. As he says, it is the study of relatively healthy individuals that resulted in the new emphasis on people's responsibilities and commitments.

In any event, we should be able to assume in T-groups that we are working with competent, healthy individuals who will become more competent and who will feel freed (not forced) to reassess their attitudes, skills, beliefs, and behaviors. Thus they may come to experience and use the T-group as an opportunity to confirm trust, openness, risk-taking, and interdependence as ways of relating to others for problem-solving and planned change activities outside the laboratory also. This is not easily accomplished but ought to be more and more possible as we learn to create healthy climates.

What is needed are more experimental tests of a proactive theory of motivation, such as Maslow's, which seek to create conditions wherein this growth predisposition of man can be engaged. Thus rather than seeking to create anxiety and regression, we need to refocus our efforts to create opportunities. As Argyris (1969) writes, if we create conditions which require survival tactics, then these well-practiced tactics will be used. We will never examine creative behaviors if we do not create conditions which at least allow, and preferably encourage, such behavior. Certainly we shall need relatively conflict-free trainers; hopefully, we can expect relatively conflict-free participants. Even though many trainers accept and identify with a proactive rather than with a reactive philosophy and psychology, their own education, training, and practice predisposes them to act automatically in the more traditional ways, as illustrated in the following list:

Some Key Phrases and Concepts Which Help to Differentiate
Two Views of Man and Human Nature

Traditional Orientation	Alternative Orientation
homeostatic model	self-realization model
reductionism	pluralism
scarcity	abundance
the way things are	the way things could be
"D" motivation	"B" motivation
therapy	reeducation

unconscious, crippling conflict	healthy, competent, problem-solving
adjustment	deviance as a positive value
reactive	proactive
central power	shared leadership
authority	social contract
survival	optimal quality of life
conflicted: regression	conflict-free: problem-solving
competition	collaboration
society	community
anxiety reduction leads to learning	dilemma-seeking: seek increases in tension
dissonance reduction	risk-taking
Argyris Type A behavior	Argyris Type B behavior
Theory X—McGregor	Theory Y—McGregor
Freud	Maslow
external locus of control	internal locus of control
role-related behavior interpersonally	increased level of aspiration in interpersonal relations
management	self-control, responsibility
transference	transfer of learning
habit	intentionality

It will take much conscious examination of attitudes and behaviors to overcome these reactions. (Others intentionally behave in traditional help-giving ways but still call what they are doing a T-group.)

Personal growth group trainers, with some notable exceptions, do not often integrate group experiences with explicit theoretical foundations, either for themselves or for participants. The efforts of people like J. V. Clark (1963), Gibb (1964b), and Hampden-Turner (1966) can be very helpful in providing evidence, other than experiential validity, for this other view of human nature and how relationships between people might be.

We might, for a moment, consider Argyris's distinctions between Type A and Type B behavior to think about how the learning climate will need to be different and what differences in behavior we might anticipate. Argyris (1969) discussed at some length "the incompleteness of social-psychological theory" and made a strong case for creating "artificial" opportunities for healthy, competent behaviors to be engaged. This takes setting up different learning environments from those usually found (such as T-groups for example). He distinguishes between A behavior and B behavior: the former, behavior which is *usual* under everyday conditions; the latter, behavior which is *possible* under other conditions. He rejects, however, the notion that what is usual is therefore natural, that is, a reflection of the nature of human nature, just as Maslow has suggested that we must set the measure of people higher.

Argyris reports an interesting study in which twenty-eight working groups in ten organizations were observed from three to twenty times for periods ranging from two months to two years, and almost 50,000 units of behavior were recorded at 163 meetings. In Table 2 can be seen the categories of behavior used for analysis. Sample statements and scores for each category are reproduced also. He draws the following conclusions which are relevant for us to consider at this time: "To conclude: We found in the 'typical world' (Pattern A), minimal openness to feelings and minimal risk-taking with ideas or feelings. The most frequently observed norms were concern for ideas (not feelings), and conformity (ideas). The norm of mistrust also tended to be high (but had to be inferred from other data . . . since individuals did not tend to show their mistrust openly)" (Argyris, 1969, p. 898). In summary, Argyris found that about 95 percent of the units of behavior recorded could be classified under six of the categories, none of them an expression of feelings. Rarely did individuals express feelings, were they open to them, nor did they experiment with ideas or feelings, except in the case of mistrust. Rarely did individuals help each other do this; neither did they do it for themselves. This he calls Pattern A. On the other hand, "pattern B groups . . . may be characterized as groups in which feelings are expressed and risks are taken; in which helping others to own, to be open, and to experiment occurs; and in which the norms of conformity and antagonism become less potent while the norms of individuality

Table 2. CATEGORIES OF BEHAVIOR

LEVEL 1						LEVEL 2	
Individual			*Interpersonal*			*Norms*	
Experimenting	i		Help others to	i		Trust	i
	f		experiment	f			f
Openness	i		Help others to	i		Concern	i
	f		be open	f			f
Owning	i		Help others to	i		Individuality	i
	f		own	f			f
			Zero line				
Not owning	i		Not help others	i		Conformity	i
	f		to own	f			f
Not open	i		Not help others	i		Antagonism	i
	f		to be open	f			f
Rejecting	i		Not help others	i		Mistrust	i
experimenting	f		to experiment	f			f

Note: Categories above zero line are hypothesized to facilitate interpersonal relationships, those below the line to inhibit interpersonal relationships. Each category has an idea (i) and a feeling (f) component. Categories positioned closest to zero line are easiest to perform and those farthest away the most difficult.

These are two levels of analyses. Level I represents the individual and interpersonal. Level II represents norms of the group. Every unit of behavior is scored on both levels. *For example:*

Sample Statement		*Would be Scored as*	
1. I believe that we should reject the idea even though we are told not to.	own i	individuality i	
2. I feel tense.	own f	individuality f	
3. Would you please tell me more about your theory?	open i	concern i	
4. This is not easy for me to talk about. I feel like my whole life has been a shambles. I feel frightened and bewildered.	experimenting f	trust f	

SOURCE: Chris Argyris, "The Incompleteness of Social Psychological Theory," *American Psychologist,* 24 (1969), p. 894.

and trust become more potent" (Argyris, 1969, p. 898). In the T-groups he observed B behavior did occur, but this is still only one part of what goes on: *i* too is present, and in high percentages. Furthermore, and this is very important to note, not all so-called T-groups become effective, and indeed by Argyris's scoring only a minority develop into Pattern B. So it is not easy to create this learning climate, nor can it be assumed by calling something a T-group. Nevertheless creating a climate with psychological safety, one where trust is possible, would seem to be a prerequisite for effective training programs, if indeed we are concerned with offering an alternative model for human relations.

It should be added that it is not enough to respond to feelings only; we must combine feelings and ideas. The T-group legitimizes acknowledging and dealing with feelings in the here-and-now. That is only one task of training. The rest of the laboratory needs to help participants conceptualize and integrate facts with feelings, to understand as well as to experience. Now we may return to look at what the T-group and the laboratory, an alternative model, look like in more detail as we join a hypothetical group.

"Good evening; my name is Ben Jordan. We will be meeting together for the next two weeks in this T-group. What happens is pretty much up to us; there is nothing already planned. This is a kind of laboratory for finding out about ourselves and about groups. Our own behavior, our feelings, our reactions, our thoughts, our relationships, our decisions—these are what we shall examine and try to understand as we go on meeting together. I am not the chairman or the teacher—although I am here to help us understand what is happening. As I look around, I realize we really have begun our life together, and I feel excited about that."

With such an introduction, a group of strangers meeting together in some isolated location may begin a short experimental life together which will rarely last more than two weeks. Ben Jordan is a trainer meeting with a T-group during a two-week training laboratory. During this period, about forty hours will be spent in T-groups by the participants who have come to this laboratory with all kinds of expectations, fears, and hopes, both explicit and implicit. Their schedule for the first week will look approximately like the one shown in Table 3.

Table 3. A T-Group Time Schedule, One Week

Time	Sunday	Monday	Tuesday	Wednesday	Thursday	Friday	Saturday
8:40– 9:00		dyad	dyad	dyad	dyad	dyad	free
9:00–11:00		T-group	T-group	T-group	T-group	T-group	free
11:00–11:30		coffee	coffee	coffee	coffee	coffee	free
11:30–12:30		theory session	theory session	theory session	theory session	theory session	free
12:30– 2:00		lunch	lunch	lunch	lunch	lunch	free
2:00– 4:00		T-group	T-group	exercise	exercise	T-group	free
4:00– 6:30	opening research	free	free	free	free	free	free
6:30– 8:00	dinner	dinner	dinner	dinner	dinner	free	free
8:00–10:00	T-group	T-group	training film	exercise	T-group	free	free
10:00–12:00	social	social	social	social	social	free	free

One way to learn about what happens in a situation is to experience it. Thus one way to learn about T-groups and other human relation activities is to participate in them. But to be only a participant is to miss a great deal of what is going on. And so it is that one of the important learnings in training groups is how to be a *participant-observer,* that is, to be in the situation and also to be able to look at it, analyze it, and understand it better; to be able to conceptualize as well as feel it.

To read about such events is another familiar way, albeit vicarious, of trying to understand but certainly it is not a sufficient way to understand interpersonal relations. Even typed transcripts of group meetings miss much of the emotional climate, obviously. So we need to invent the *participant-observer-reader.* It would be a good idea, therefore, for the reader to create opportunities to experience some of the situations described here as an integral part of his or her learning. Sometimes, therefore, we suggest that the reader stop to reflect on past personal experiences which are relevant, or to examine his own behavior. It is important to share actively in these experiences if the reader wishes to *know* as well as *know about* T-groups. Perhaps at this point the reader could pause to think about some recent group experiences and reflect on some critical incidents, that is, situations in which something important did or did not happen: in a classroom, on a committee, at a staff meeting, and so forth. Now select one which you recall with pleasure and satisfaction and another which you recall with distress and dissatisfaction. Can you think of some things that made them so different? What was the group trying to accomplish in each case? Was it done? What feelings come to mind as you reflect on each situation? Can you recall any dialogue with individuals in the group? (Write down an exchange you had with one or more individuals in each case.) In retrospect, what would you do now if you had it to do over again? What would be the ideal solution as you see it?

Human relations training experiences, that is, T-groups and laboratory training, are a deliberate, supervised attempt to experience and understand such differences; to make it possible for interpersonal relations to be more satisfying emotionally and for groups of individuals to work together more effectively. And to understand what facilitates and what impedes this process. To get a good idea of what a three-week laboratory experience is like, see Marrow's *Behind the Executive Mask* (1964); for some understanding of personal growth and encounter groups, see Howard's *Please Touch* (1971). For further contrast, see *Marathon 16* (Shepard and Lee, 1971). All these books include verbatim accounts as well as general descriptions.

In the deceptively simple words of Miles (1959), we can define a trainer as "a person with special responsibility for helping individuals learn from their experiences." He does this intentionally through his interventions, that is, by deliberate attempts to focus attention on what is going on in the here-and-now so that the participants will develop increased awareness and learn to be more effective participant-observers (by being able to be both intensely involved and able to analyze the process). Participants will come expecting a teacher, a leader, a staff person who will direct the activities. Instead, they will need to learn to look to themselves and each other as resources. The trainer will have to convey how this new collaborative venture works by being a unique member whose functions will be taken over by others. From the very first meeting, the effort to demonstrate this alternative model, to live it, begins.

It is important to reiterate that what is the most important learning that can be transferred is *learning how to learn,* an attitude of openness, a problem-solving approach. In many groups this is often forgotten in the emotional prominence of a particular experience: an encounter, a dramatic change, a painful or joyous moment. True, there can be "immediate learning," that is, traumatic conversions from not understanding to understanding. However, even Corsini (1970), working as a therapist who arranges powerfully emotional situations, tells us that this works for about one in three patients, and in any case it takes place in an ongoing group. The less dramatic but more lasting learning under personal control—to know and experience and be able to recognize that emotion and intellect affect each other; to learn that we all send mixed messages and receive others' messages through our own distorting filters; to find ways of identifying when this is happening; and how we can intervene constructively in those processes—this is a truly collaborative venture in interpersonal and group effectiveness which not only utilizes the special skills of the trainer but allows the participant to go away stronger, more effective, and not dependent on the magic of the trainer or the group and yet able to acknowledge their importance in these learnings.

An example for immediate therapy is "the therapist attempts to drive the patient to a climax of emotionalism, and then when he thinks he has gotten to the farthest point, suddenly stops the action and sends the patient out of the group . . . (the) 're-construction phase' is diminished if the patient is permitted to stay in the group. For this reason, as soon as the subject has achieved this raw emotional climax, regardless of how upset he is, he must be sent out of the group. 'Nursing' or other forms of sympathy must not be permitted. The reconstruction is done alone" (Corsini, 1970, p. 30).

An example from a T-group is:

It took this kind of permissive atmosphere to bring my deep-est feelings to the surface—and give me an idea of the kind of person I really am.

What happened was that the first things people told me about myself were negative, and the first things I told them about myself were always positive. Then as we got to know one another better, I began to recognize some of the negative things they found in me, and they began to find some positive qualities I didn't even know I possessed.

The second week got down to cases even faster. That's when I learned that unless I was willing to stick my neck out, I was going to have to give up any hopes of a leadership posi-tion in the T-group because I had nothing to offer. My team-mates saw me as a guy who could be moved in either direction. Suddenly a lot of things that had happened to me back on the job fell into place. Just a couple of months before I had missed out on an important promotion. Now I know why.

But it was the third week that really got to me. The day I was dropped by my team as one of the least valuable mem-bers, I cried. It was that old bugaboo again—I didn't stand for anything. I hated those guys at first, but I've got to admit they had me down pat.

I'm going back home now. I know what I've got to work on

—and work on it I will. I understand myself better. It was
a salutary shock to hear the group verdict to oust me. I knew
then they saw me for the person I was—but I pretended I
was not.
I feel confident I now have the courage and the competence
to know myself without distortion of partiality (Marrow,
1964, p. 33).

It is assumed that some members have the necessary leadership skills, although the effective trainer will have a broad range of
skills. Whether seen as catalyst, role model, sphinx, interventionist,
or guru, the trainer is a central figure in the training group as he
shares his skills, knowledge, attitudes, values, experiences, and self
with the other members of the group. However, he is a unique
member who should become more and more dispensable in his
role. As Jenkins (1967) points out, a trainer's behavior is his tool
of work; it is intentional behavior. It is his job to select methods
which will accomplish the purposes of training and which will not
have side consequences that go against the human values which the
trainer holds in the situation. It is impossible to talk about democratic training except as operating through a set of values about
human beings which is held and lived by the trainer. Good interventions are those which intentionally create learning opportunities
which are then used. No trainer is perfect, that is, he can only
work toward intentional, helpful consequences. Obviously all opportunities cannot be capitalized on, so timing and selection become
important skills of the trainer. All these interactions become more
and more natural and spontaneous with experience, that is, as
knowledge and skills become more and more integrated with the
trainer's values and attitudes.

As the group progresses, trainer interventions should be
assumed more and more by members. These interventions are of
three general types: as either an observer or as an interpreter of
events in the group; as a member, contributing his own feelings
and behavior; and as a source of resources, he may suggest or introduce ways of data collection and study (Bradford, 1964, p. 213).
Theoretically at least, all of these functions can be assumed by the
members, collectively, and there can thus be true shared leadership

in such a group experience. However, the trainer should be working out of some learning theory frame of reference; he will have formulated some theory of change and will have a more rather, than a less, explicitly formulated set of values. This belief in the values and metagoals of the laboratory should be apparent in his behavior.

In a training group, the trainer is not a "projection screen." Instead, he deliberately helps move the group to peer-related interdependence, and is himself seen as a fellow human being. The trainer's member-like behaviors contribute: "(1) to an attentuation of transference reactions and to diminished preoccupation with the central figure, (2) to a decrease in regressive reactions, and (3) to increased interaction and interdependence among the members. To achieve the goal of maximum learning about blind spots and distortions in one's personal interactions in a brief time-limited group—the 'member-like' role of the trainer seems preferable to the transference role of the therapist" (Horwitz, 1964b, p. 212).

Gertz (1969) has shown how the same event can be turned to a therapy or a training purpose; in the former case by there-and-then interpretation, that is, taking it outside the group; in the latter case by here-and-now analysis, that is, seeing its significance in this group. As he suggests, there are probably critical incidents which can help the group go either way—become a therapy group or remain a T-group. He suggests that we need to look carefully at what the members do, what effects this has on the group, what the trainer does, what are his goals, and what are the consequences. We are suggesting that trainers need a philosophy as well as a training style and that interventions reflect and serve both.

More and more people are willing and eager to have a group experience known variously as sensitivity training, human relations laboratory, an experiential group, a training group, a workshop, and classically as a T-group. It is often an experience they approach with excitement, a sense of anticipated pleasure mixed with anxiety, and leave with a variety of emotions, usually positive. According to Bennis, there are probably three million people who have had some such related experience; according to Harris (1970), perhaps six million. Still, like being born, falling in love, and dying, it is often difficult for the participants to articulate the nature of the experience, and they often fall back on the cliche "you can't really know what it means until you have been through it."

What is supposed to be happening has been perhaps most clearly articulated by Bradford (1964). He describes four major purposes of group experience training: learning how to learn, learning how to give help, developing effective membership, and becoming sensitive to group processes. It is perhaps easier in this context to understand why an individual with only one group experience will not have mastered all of these learnings well enough to share them but nevertheless may have acquired some skill in one or more group experiences. We can see then that learning may need to take place over a period of time, on several occasions. In addition, these may not be the member's goals when he comes.

Learning how to learn is one of the immediate and central goals of laboratory training. This means acquiring, for the time being at least, an orientation which incorporates the democratic and scientific metagoals of the training experience: *a spirit of inquiry; collaboration; authenticity; expanded consciousness; and an awareness of, and the use of, more options in behavior.* This is not an easy task. The group consists of people who have come to learn but bring with them many years of experiences, habits, attitudes, and behaviors which make them likely to respond in their usual ways. How shall it be arranged that they can experiment or even want to experiment? How will they learn to be sensitive to cues which they have long ignored or misread: their internal emotional cues, nonverbal cues from others, all the hidden agenda items, and so forth? How to create a learning environment which engages proactive behavior, which promotes growth?

The member must come with some readiness to experiment with his interpersonal behavior repertoire if he is to learn from his group experience. This readiness can be latent; that is to say, participants may be getting on very satisfactorily with their present strategies for relating at work and at home in routine ways. But, given either the opportunity or the necessity for examining those usual patterns, they should be able to examine and discard old patterns and risk trying out new ones and also be able to look at the consequences of these new patterns and make intentional choices. Members need to care about the group as well as themselves. They must also be facilitators, that is, they must help others to contribute. They need to recognize the importance of sharing their own feelings about decisions being made and norms being established. They ought to be able to support the decisions arrived at because they have truly had an opportunity to share in them. "Basically the purpose of the laboratory is to free people to view the groups they work in as dynamic entities, and to find ways of understanding and influencing the directions in which these changes can/should take place" (Jenkins, 1967, p. 3).

Schein and Bennis (1965) suggest we consider these as L-groups, which are defined as controlled learning environments where people can learn about interpersonal, small group, and organizatioal relations so that they can make better choices, that is, so that their intentions and their behavior can become more congruent. There will be practice in diagonsis, and what is learned is a spirit of inquiry coupled with knowledge and skills.

It will be recalled that laboratory training education is a method for providing people with the opportunity to explore and experiment with interpersonal behavior and group problem-solving by creating a temporary society in which all data about relating and problem-solving and building a group are available to all. All history starts now. It is in the T-group that the more usual expectations of the participants about what groups are about can be confronted.

The special kind of inquiry that will be taking place centers around process analysis: what is happening and how can we understand what is going on? The activities that are required for being in the group seem simple enough: participation, observation, listening, responding, analyzing, trying out some new (for them) behaviors, seeing what happens. There really are no novel or mysterious things going on. Indeed one of the important learnings is to recognize that it is possible to understand interpersonal and group interactions and to be able to bring intentions and effects closer together. To do this, people must begin to pay attention to cues which ordinarily are ignored; to become conscious of many stimuli which they have learned to ignore over time. Increased awareness is one of the fundamental objectives. Along with increased awareness are many new possibilities for action that present themselves, resulting in more options to choose from. How choices are made will come to be understood better also.

From the moment that the T-group comes together for the first time, the history of the group has begun; everything that happens becomes data; what each person and the group does and does not do or say is up for scrutiny. All the usual trappings or role-related behaviors are abolished: informal clothing and first names are in order. There is no agenda. The other parts of the laboratory training will help by way of lectures, skill exercises, and perhaps a notebook neatly summarizing some behavioral science findings and theoretical formulations about groups. But in the meeting room are all the ingredients for the drama that will unfold: people and time and self-conscious exploration. What will be learned? What can be taken away? What are the objectives?

After the trainer has made his introductory remarks at the first meeting, participants attempt to make some sense out of what is happening. Some deal with the trainer, some with each other, a few sit back and wait. Often, all conversation is recorded on a tape recorder, and individuals (perhaps the entire group) will want to listen later on; the sessions may even be videotaped. The trainer begins to establish his place—to show who he is—and he begins to know who the participants are. In everyday life, roles are usually defined for everyone. Here the members can try out different ways of behaving: there are no usual expectations. How will each person establish his membership? How will each deal with the leader?

By the end of the first session, there is a sense of excitement; the possibilities of the experience begin to be felt by many. Perhaps already someone has said: "I think this is going to be an opportunity for me to face up to who I really am," and in an I-Thou moment, everyone felt related to that possibility. The others present begin to be personally important. Or perhaps the trainer already has said to a participant: "I'm not sure I really understood what you just said to me. Let me repeat what I heard, and you can tell me if that is what you said." Thus a lesson in learning to listen is underway. Each participant could check out his version of what he heard to see how close it was to the message received by the trainer and the message the participant will now say he intended to send.

Learning how to learn has begun. Participants will compare

reactions after the meeting with those in their group, and, for now, with those in other groups. In another session or two, members of other groups will be seen as outsiders. Trainers, too, will compare their reactions and begin to reconsider the design: how well will it suit these individuals, these groups? What expectations have they brought?

By the second or third session, feedback to the trainer may become very hostile. How he accepts such feedback at this time is very important to the group and may greatly influence the norm that is set for dealing with conflict. Now, as often, the trainer is sustained by his faith in the process, by his skills, and perhaps by his colleagues. Meanwhile, members are learning how to identify and deal with their feelings. They are learning how they are perceived and how their intentions and the effects of their behavior differ. They may begin to experiment with behaving in new ways: talking more than usual or less than usual; meeting their own needs, their feelings of not knowing what to do by withdrawing; or moving in to help with the work of the group.

What can this group of people do together that is important? What is getting in the way? From the beginning, decisions are being made and norms are being set—often implicitly. They will need to focus on how this is happening—the trainer's interventions will help them to do this. To be self-managing, however, the members will have to take responsibility themselves for stopping the action to look at the process: to learn to observe and to analyze. If things get bogged down, how can they change the situation? One thing they will learn will be how to do a "force field analysis," that is, to recognize the driving and restraining forces operating to create a problem or to keep it from being resolved.

In the T-group, it is important for participants to try to understand, to make sense out of what is going on, as well as to be experiencing emotionally. The trainer helps in this search through his interventions, which are deliberate attempts to focus on important learnings; through personal feedback; and through his own responses. Improved observation methods are needed by the participants, and opportunities are designed to achieve this objective. Many messages are sent and received; not all are intentional. Members must learn how to deal with double messages and with distortions which they put on the messages. Feedback is a central and critical process, and the closer in time it occurs to the event being responded to, the better. Increased self-awareness is an important learning. Discrepancies between intentions and effects should be looked into carefully.

Much of the training centers around becoming more aware of, and understanding better, what is going on: intrapersonally, interpersonally, and intergroup. Schein (1969) has written about process consultation. Although he focuses on organization development, the processes he selects to focus on will serve as a good frame of reference for looking at how groups work in more detail. These processes include communication, member roles and functions in groups, group problem-solving and decision-making, group norms and group growth, leadership and authority, and intergroup cooperation and competition.

As participants behave, observe, analyze, and evaluate, they will ask many questions: How are decisions made, or why are they not made? Is it in generating ideas or carrying them out that the group falters? How is leadership distributed—is it authority-centered or is it collaborative? Are there leadership functions which are not being met? How do individual needs get met? How do individuals find a place or gain membership in the group? How do the tasks get done and how is the group itself maintained? Who communicates with whom, and how? What could be done to improve communication? How are norms established, and around what kinds of issues? Are the norms mostly implicit or explicit? How competitive or collaborative are groups with each other? Integrally mingled with these thoughts, observations, and activities will be all kinds of feelings: clear and unclear, old and new. There will be fear and anger and rage; there will be exhilaration and joy and love; there will be feelings of inadequacy and confusion and feelings of insight and clarity; there will be loneliness and there will be belongingness. And often the feelings will be strong enough to blot out any understanding.

Through observation, trainer interventions, exercises, conceptual material, and analysis of the experiences and evaluations of planned changes, such questions are addressed. Which questions are asked and how well they are answered varies from group to group. Hopefully, for most people the feelings and the thoughts will begin to fit together, and an individual will find that his increased awareness and increased options free him to sort his values, set priorities, and act with conviction. Always, time is limited—and what can be done in the time available.

Communication

There are many ways to look at the communication process in a group. At a very simple observational level, one can count the number of times each person speaks. Beyond that, a record can be kept of the pattern of communication: who speaks to whom, after whom, and so forth. An interaction diagram helps to tally this information for any time sample period. For example, three five-minute samples during a one and a half hour meeting of a committee might show that only three of the ten people present spoke more than once; two spoke only to each other, and the third addressed each member at some time; the others simply spoke to no one in particular. Added to this observation could be the total length of time each person uses and the pattern of interruptions. At the descriptive level, it is merely interesting; however, looking for patterns, changes over time, or analyzing for meaning, lead to much richer use of data. Checking out hypotheses about the meanings inferred leads to modification or confirmation of these conjectures. There are also accompanying correlates: tone of voice, silences, postures, and so forth, which usually are interpreted implicitly by participants; these private perceptions normally do not get checked out in any public way in back-home situations.

However, in the T-group, this is part of the feedback process—a process in which people share their private perceptions and can compare them with others who are experiencing the same event. One of the more useful ways of understanding some of the ways in which communication is complicated is called The Johari Window (Luft, 1963, pp. 10–15)` which is a four-part analysis of the communication process. It suggests that there are: (1) some things we do and say which we wish to do and say; this we can call our *free* area of activity, or our *open* self. There are (2)` some things we purposely hide or try to hide; this we can call our *hidden* or *concealed* self. Then there are (3) some things we do and say which we do not know we are doing, that is, we are sending messages we do not intend to send, something we can call our *blind* area—but other people can hear and see these messages. Finally there are (4) some messages we do not know we are sending, of which we are unaware; and these are received by others who do not understand them either, for they are *unconscious* behaviors, that is, those sent and received without awareness.

T-groups are concerned with the first three kinds of behavior, and it is assumed that given a psychologically safe environment and people who are intentionally paying concerned attention to themselves and to each other, the area of free and open communication will increase and the areas of hidden and blind behavior will grow smaller. Our blind self is helped by feedback; our hidden self will grow smaller. Our blind self is helped by feedback; our hidden self is freed by a change in the restraining forces, a safer environment. Thus the area of free and open communication can increase greatly and encourage much freer and more authentic communication and less likelihood of distortion, intentional or unintentional. Therefore, increased awareness can lead to changed attitudes which in turn can lead to improved interpersonal competence. In this environment in which a group of strangers come to be concerned for and value each other, all are confirmed in their complexity as well as in their commonalities. Schein (1969, p. 24) has modified the Johari Window by showing a two-person interaction, with the "windows" of each person in communication at various levels. (The size or importance of each "window" varies, depending on the individual and the situation in interaction. See Figure 1.)

Usually people are put into stereotyped categories by others and are kept there on the basis of very little data (for example, sex, race, size, or tone of voice). We come to conclusions about what someone will say, and we do not bother to hear what he says but hear instead what we think he said. Again, feedback is a way to check out these inpressions as the participants all share their perceptions of the same event. Simple exercises, such as the following listening exercise from Pfeiffer and Jones (1969, pp. 31–34), achieve the same result:

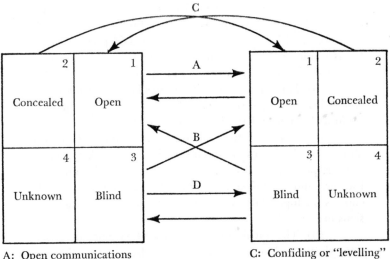

A: Open communications
B: Leakage or unwitting revelations

C: Confiding or "levelling"
D: Emotional contagion

FIGURE 1.   Types of Messages in a Two-Person Communication Situation. Based on Edgar H. Schein, *Process Consultation: Its Role in Organization Development* (Menlo Park, Calif.: Addison-Wesley, 1969), Figure 3.2, p. 24.

Goal: To understand the necessity of listening to each other accurately as opposed to merely hearing words without comprehension.

Group size: Unlimited number of triads.

Time required: Approximately forty-five minutes.

Materials utilized: (1) Topics for Discussion sheets for each triad. (2) Questions for Discussion sheets for each triad.

Physical setting: Triads will separate from one another to avoid outside noise interference.

Process: (1) Triads are formed. (2) Participants in each triad number themselves A, B, or C. (3) The facilitator distributes Topics for Discussion sheets. (4) In each group, one person will act as referee and the other two as participants in a discussion of one of the topics found on the sheet. One will be the speaker and the other the listener.

(5) The following instructions are given by the facili-

tator: (A) The discussion is to be unstructured except that before each participant speaks, he must first summarize, in his own words, without notes, what has been said previously. (B) If his summary is thought to be incorrect, the speaker or the referee are free to interrupt and clear up any misunderstanding.

(6) Participant A begins as speaker. He is allowed to choose his own topic from those listed. (7) Participant B will begin as listener and participant C as referee.

(8) The discussion progresses as follows: (A) After about seven minutes of discussion by the speaker and the listener, participant B becomes the speaker, participant C the listener, and participant A the referee. The new speaker chooses his topic. (B) After another seven minutes the discussions are halted.

(9) The facilitator distributes Questions for Discussions sheets and conducts a discussion based upon the questions.

Topics for discussion (choose one topic): (1) Inter-racial and inter-faith marriages—good or bad? Why? (2) Pre-marital sex relations—acceptable or not? Why? (3) Should college students be eligible for the draft? (4) Is the U. S. right in its Vietnam policies? (5) Should the number of required credits be reduced? (6) Black Power—good or bad for Blacks? (7) Are student activists justified in taking over college buildings? (8) (Any other contemporary issue may be substituted.)

Questions for discussion: (1) Did you find that you had difficulty in listening to others during the exercise? Why? (2) Did you find that you had difficulty in formulating your thoughts and listening at the same time? (a) Forgetting what you were going to say. (b) Not listening to others. (c) Rehearsing your response.

(3) When others paraphrased your remarks, did they do it in a shorter, more concise way? (4) Did you find that you were not getting across what you wanted to say? (5) Was the manner of presentation by others affecting your listening ability? (Pfeiffer and Jones, 1969, pp. 31–34).

Feedback should be behavior-specific, nonjudgmental, and given as close in time to the event as possible. It should be confirmed or modified by all others present so as to be of maximum use to the recipient. It should be something the recipient can do something about. It is not a way of letting off steam, that is, expressive behavior for the sender. It should be about something which everyone in the group has shared so that all can share in the feedback process. *Not everything someone says to another member is feedback,* and not all feedback is "good" feedback. As Kolb and Boyatzis (1970, p. 274) say: "most learning theorists have concluded that in the long run reward is more effective than punishment. One example of reward-centered feedback is found in the programmed instruction technique of 'error-free learning.' Rogers, too, places heavy emphasis on the importance of positive feedback to the client in his concept of unconditional positive regard."

Fink (1968) suggests that the "raw data" of a T-group are the immediate reactions (thoughts or feelings) of the group members to one another. Further, if interpersonal communications (that is, feedback) contain these raw data, a positive group climate will develop whereas interpretations and abstractions lead to negative group climate and inhibit the learning process. Therefore, if the trainer is to be a role model, he cannot reserve interpretations and abstractions for himself, while encouraging communication of raw data in members. For one thing, interpretations can lead to a false sense of insight, and in addition the receiver needs to know what the effects of his intentions are on other people: do they want to come closer, go farther away, resist him, and so forth. The raw data need not be feelings: they can be metaphors, fantasies, or thoughts, but they are not interpretations. They are here-and-now reactions and belong in the experience. They also allow the receiver to know what effects he is having on various people. Although the trainer does have special skills, which he shares, he should be willing to share his human reactions also, as raw data.

Some examples of feedback are:

(1) Joan, your silence scares me. You seem so cool. You hardly ever speak and never say anything stupid or critical, and I begin to feel more stupid and more uncool. Are you waiting for us to say something worth your attention, or are you really just too scared to speak?

(2) Do you know that you've been talking for seven minutes by the clock, Paul? I feel as if I'm going to explode. I'm mad at you, I'm mad at myself, and I'm mad at everyone else for letting it happen.

(3) I feel as if I've just been given a command instead of an invitation, Joe. My first reaction is to say "no" even though I want to do it. Your posture, your voice, your abruptness all make me feel challenged.

(4) I like what you just said, Tom; you helped clear up my confusion, and I felt you cared for me personally as well. You do that often, you know—help clarify an idea without making the other person feel foolish or threatened.

(5) I'd be angry if he had said that to me, Anne. What are you feeling? I thought I heard a hint of your wanting support but I can't tell from your words or your expression, and I don't know what to do next.

All of these examples give the receiver of the feedback information about his impact on the sender and express the sender's feelings. They are based on behavior that is current and has been witnessed by all of the participants so they can share their reactions with the sender and the receiver, and they relate to behaviors that can be changed if the receiver so desires. Argyris (1968) also points out that feedback should not be in terms of inferences but should be minimally evaluative, minimally contradictory, directly verifiable, and descriptive of the impact the sender is having on one's self. The receiver offers his reactions and his perceptions, and the silence of any member is viewed as nonconstructive since feedback is important. Even in our everyday lives, feedback shapes us into what we are; at its worst, it can "drive us crazy" (Laing, 1971), by forcing us to distort our first-hand experiences. It is very important to learn how to give and receive less distorted feedback if we are to have meaningful communication.

Discrepancies between an individual's intentions and effects should not be glossed over since it is in this way that "unfreezing" can occur (Nadler, 1969; Schein and Bennis, 1965). In order for behavior to change the individual must want to to change and feel himself capable of change. This means that he must trust both himself and others enough to give up certain familiar patterns. His actions can also be confirmed by others so that he can continue to do those things.

Member Roles and Functions in Groups

As was said in the previous section, people often are circumscribed by others: that is, they are given limited roles in the groups in which they live and work, and their repertoire of participation activities is narrowly defined. People come to accept their roles and to behave in expected ways. Many, if not most, relationships are role-related rather than person-to-person. The many possibilities any individual has for perhaps endless complexity and variety are never given a chance. It has been said that therapy is the reorganization of the individual; training can be viewed as the reconsideration of role-related behavior. How shall the individual see these limitations?

In order to know how he himself is functioning, and perhaps how other people are functioning, observing is one of the first skills a participant must improve. Even more difficult is learning to be a participant-observer—to be fully functioning in the group and yet able to watch the process. This can be done artificially by stepping out of the group and taking turns as a process observer. In the early days of T-groups, a staff member performed that function in order to be able to give feedback at the end of the session. The role of process observer should become a skill which can be practiced much of the time in the natural situation of the group interaction. In this case, it would become synonymous with being a participant-observer. Observing can be informal and undirected, that is, the individual can simply look, listen, and let whatever will come to his attention. In that case we may distort impressions in an idiosyncratic way, according to our own needs and filters. Another method is directed observation, that is, to look at what is going on in a systematic, predetermined way, for example, to check off on a list, enter observations into categories, take verbatim records at predetermined intervals, and so forth.

In order to see what is going on in a group, it is often useful to examine how the necessary functions are being performed. This method of looking at groups was originally suggested by Benne and Sheats (1948) and suggests that there are three kinds of inter-actions: those that are helpful for the work or task of the group; those that are helpful for the maintenance or growth of the group itself; and those that are not very helpful to the group qua group, that is, that serve individual purposes. Eleven helpful roles were identified, and it is assumed that these are necessary at various times if the group is to function effectively. Four nonfunctional roles were also identified (see Table 4).

An analysis of what is happening in a group may reveal that some or many roles are not being taken, or that a few individuals are engaged in a good deal of nonfunctional (for the group) behavior. The T-group is a good place for members to practice some of these tasks and maintenance roles which are ordinarily not in their repertoire but are necessary for effective groups. Increased role flexibility will make them more useful members in other groups as well, and they may deliberately set some learning goals for themselves around participation in the T-group.

One way to observe would be to record interactions at regular intervals, for example, the first five minutes every half hour. Obviously, it could then be seen how each individual is participating; or the recording could be done by category to see which functions are not being met without regard to individual contributions. Categorizing a comment takes some skill and practice, something that can be taught as part of the training program. Practice in the needed roles can also be built in, and this learning can be transferred. Participants are more likely to be skilled in task roles and will need to learn maintenance roles. They also are likely to be using a limited number of roles in their usual group associations. Increasing their role flexibility, combined with knowing when certain functions seem necessary, are important and transferrable learnings. If there is much nonfunctional behavior, it is not necessarily the individual's fault: It may mean that the group is not satisfying individual needs through its work. Both increased awareness and intentionality are served by these analyses and practice. A group which gives most of its attention to task roles will be less productive than a group which gives approximately equal attention to both task and group functions is an assumption which could use further testing.

Table 4. SAMPLE RECORD OF ROLES GROUP
MEMBERS MIGHT TAKE IN A SINGLE SESSION

	MEMBERS							
Task Functions	A	B	C	D	E	F	G	H
Defines problem	X						X	X
Seeks information		X	X					X
Gives information			X				X	X
Seeks opinions		X		X				
Gives opinions	X		X				X	X
Tests feasibility	X	X					X	

Group Building and
Maintenance Functions

	A	B	C	D	E	F	G	H
Coordinating	X						X	
Mediating-Harmonizing								
Orienting-Facilitating			X		X			
Supporting-Encouraging ...								X
Following			X					

Individual Functions

	A	B	C	D	E	F	G	H
Blocking	X			X			X	
Out of Field								X
Digressing	X		X				X	X
Seeking recognition		X						X

SOURCE: Hedley G. Dimock, *How to Observe Your Group* (Montreal: Sir George William University, 1970), p. 29. Based on the role-formulations of K. Benne and P. Sheats.

Another way to look at behavior in the group is to assess one's own behavior and then compare it with how one is perceived by others. For example, data in Table 5 can be used early in the group's history, and repeated later, to look for changes both in intention and in effects. Members can set learning goals on the basis of how they are, how they are perceived, and how they would like to be. (It is important to recognize that the technology for observation, evaluation, and so forth, is used as a means, not as an end in itself. There is much spontaneous interaction; yet there is increased opportunity to build in more intentional outcomes if there is also more intentional analysis.)

All kinds of arts, crafts, sciences, and sports consider advanced training or refresher courses to be appropriate. But to consider that there are human relations skills that can be understood or practiced normally requires that one be a child, and therefore being socialized; or "sick," and therefore being resocialized. However, in human relations laboratories, individuals may discover that choice rather than chance is another way of looking at the everyday world and their relationships in that world; and planned change, variability, and intentionality may come to replace role and ritual.

Group Problem-Solving and Decision-Making

Identifying a problem often turns out to be the most difficult part of problem-solving. One way to find out what it is, is to do a problem census: that is, make a list, either private or public, in which everyone contributes his version of what the problem is or what the problems are. Before there can be a solution, there must be some kind of agreement on what the problem is, or on setting priorities about problem-solving if there is more than one problem —as there surely will be.

Another way to move on might be to do a *force field analysis:* that is, having once identified the problem, the members of the group will want to identify the restraining forces and the driving forces that are maintaining the situation. A useful way of thinking about change was proposed by Kurt Lewin, who saw behavior as a dynamic balance of forces working in opposite directions. Whatever

Table 5. Analysis of My Behavior in Groups

DIRECTIONS: Place an "H" on each scale to indicate your behavior in *this* group. Now on each scale place a letter "T" to indicate your self-rating of your typical behavior in working with *other* groups. (At the end, you will find further directions.)

1. Drive to push forward my own ideas; to influence others.

0	1	2	3	4	5	6	7
No such drive			Average				Strong drive

2. Openness, frankness in expressing my own real feelings.

0	1	2	3	4	5	6	7
Repressed, disguised, masked, careful			Average				Free, open, frank, spontaneous

3. Listening to, using, building on the ideas of others.

0	1	2	3	4	5	6	7
Never do			Average				Always do

Table 5. ANALYSIS OF MY BEHAVIOR IN GROUPS (cont.)

4. Awareness of feelings of other members in the group, even when these are not being overtly expressed.

0	1	2	3	4	5	6	7
Not aware			Average				Always highly perceptive and concerned

5. My reaction to potential conflict in the group.

0	1	2	3	4	5	6	7
Seek to avoid or repress it			Average				Explore and find value in it

6. Extent of my trust in other members of the group.

0	1	2	3	4	5	6	7
None			Average				Great, genuine

7. Desire for warm, close, affectionate relations with group members.

0	1	2	3	4	5	6	7
None, prefer impersonal			Average				Strong desire

8. Ability to accept disagreement with your own ideas, and criticism of your behavior.

0	1	2	3	4	5	6	7
None, resent criticism			Average				Readily accept and often change

9. Giving encouragement, support, and appreciation to other group members.

0	1	2	3	4	5	6	7
Never do			Average				Always do this freely, generously

FURTHER DIRECTIONS:

A. What do you see as your *greatest strength* as a group member? Along which of the nine dimensions do you believe you usually make your biggest contribution to groups in which you work?

B. What *change* in your usual behavior would do most to improve your effectiveness as a good group member? Along which of the nine dimensions, in what direction, and how much change do you see as desirable?

the present status quo, it is the result of this balance; in order to change the status quo, there must be an imbalance to unfreeze the pattern. Then there can be a change, and the balance again stabilizes but in a different way. Increasing a driving force increases the tension; it is usually preferable to decrease the restraining forces. The forces have different amounts of influence; if the sum of the forces is greater for positive change, then the group can move in that direction. Obviously, this can be accomplished by weakening the restraining forces. An example of how such a force field analysis might look is included in Table 6 and Table 7. Such an analysis can be done of course for any system: an individual, a group, an organization, and so forth. Afterwards, decisions about how to go about changing the picture so that agreed-on goals can be achieved must be made, resulting in more satisfaction for individuals.

Another useful way to look at group interaction which has some relevance for this question of decision-making is the well-known Bales' Interaction Process Analysis (1950). This involves looking at six interrelated dimensions of interactions, problems related to orientation, evaluation, control, decision, tension management, and integration. The first three are task roles, the latter three are social-emotional roles. The former are either positive or negative, and the latter means either raising questions or attempting answers. The ratio of positive acts to negative acts in any area gives an idea of how much difficulty the group is having with that problem (see Table 8).

As Schein (1969) observes, the decision process itself can be handled by lack of group response, authority rule, minority rule, majority rule, and either consensus or unanimity. The logically perfect way may be unanimity, but the important thing is to agree on the method and recognize that unanimity is not always possible. Nevertheless, there can be *unanimous support* of the decision if all of the emotional difficulties have been faced and dealt with during the discussion. Thus individuals' personal emotional needs are met even if there still is disagreement around issues.

Group Norms and Group Growth

The T-group is a temporary system that starts out with no history of its own and therefore has no group norms. As the group

Table 6. FORCE FIELD ANALYSIS OF A DEPARTMENT
IN A UNIVERSITY

Driving	*Restraining*
Innovative atmosphere	Lines of communications
Freedom	Lack of time
Absence of traditional superordinate-subordinate relationship	Ego trips
Sharing of power	Too many students
Wide range of human resources	Infinitude of objectives
High expectations	Lack of priorities
Respect for value of people	Confusion between novelty and innovation
Common "enemy"	Lack of resources (human and otherwise)
Talented people	Sharing of power (who's in charge here?)
Real world orientation	Lack of mutual support
"Do your own thing"	Conflicting demands
Multiple intense commitments	Lack of information
High energy level	"Do your own thing"
Crisis orientation	Multiple intense commitments
	Fatigue
Accessibility of faculty	Lack of structures that make routine difficult
Pride in being first on the moon	Crisis orientation
Rule by men as contrasted with rule by law	Action-oriented—anti-intellectual
	Too much printed material

Table 7. Sample Force Field Analysis of Attitudes of Members Toward a T-Group

(X) *Driving individual's attraction to the group*	(Y) *Restraining individual's attraction to the group*
+50 +40 +30 +20 +10	−10 −20 −30 −40 −50
1. External: My previous experiences with T-groups. ⟶	1. External: My previous experiences with T-groups. ⟵
2. I like the way I'm listened to in this group. ⟶	2. There are members of this group who inhibit my openness. ⟵
3. This group allows me to express myself. I feel I can be myself here. ⟶	3. This group isn't run the way I feel groups should be run. ⟵
4. I like this group because the other people in the group seem to like me. (Affiliation oriented member) ⟶	4. The members of this group all seem to have things in common. I feel left out. ⟵
5. I like this group because I approve of the goals. (Achievement-oriented member) ⟶	5. The task of this group seems unimportant to me. ⟵
6. I like this group because I can influence the direction of the group (Power-oriented member). ⟶	6. No one seems interested in my suggestions for discussion topics. ⟵
7. I like this group because it satisfies the needs I bring to the group from the outside, i.e., "My supervisor wants me to join this group"). ⟶	7. The leader of this group is a real loser. ⟵

Implications of the force field analysis. For each numbered item, an arrow is drawn toward the central zero line, according to the force exerted—the longer the arrow the greater the force.

1. If X + Y is more than 0, then the person who is highly attracted to the group wants to remain in it.
2. If X + Y is less than 0, the person will want to leave the group.
3. If X + Y equals 0, the group is at a standstill, and needs to move in one direction or another, in order to heighten or lessen attraction of the group.

Table 8. INTERACTION PROCESS ANALYSIS

Behaviors			*Problems*
A. Social-Emotional Area: Positive	A.	1. *Shows solidarity,* raises other's status, gives help, reward:	f
	A.	2. *Shows tension release,* jokes, laughs, shows satisfaction:	e
	A.	3. *Agrees,* shows passive acceptance, understands, concurs, complies:	d
	B.	4. *Gives suggestion,* direction, implying autonomy for other:	c
	B.	5. *Gives opinion,* evaluation, analysis, expresses feeling, wish:	b
B., C. Task Area: Neutral	B.	6. *Gives orientation,* information, repeats, clarifies, confirms:	a
	C.	7. *Asks for orientation,* information, repetition, confirmation:	a
	C.	8. *Asks for opinion,* evaluation, analysis, expression of feeling:	b
D. Social-Emotional Area: Negative	C.	9. *Asks for suggestion,* direction, possible ways of action:	c
	D.	10. *Disagrees,* shows passive rejection, formality, withholds help:	d
	D.	11. *Shows tension,* asks for help, withdraws out of field:	e
	D.	12. *Shows antagonism,* deflates other's status, defends or asserts self:	f

A. Positive Reactions
B. Attempted Answers
C. Questions
D. Negative Reactions

a. Problems of Communication
b. Problems of Evaluation
c. Problems of Control
d. Problems of Decision
e. Problems of Tension Reduction
f. Problems of Reintegration

SOURCE: Based on R. F. Bales, *Interaction Process Analysis* (Cambridge: Addison-Wesley, 1950).

meets and acquires a history, it also acquires accepted ways of doing things. These norms probably are related to the issues important in building this group: how the trainer will be dealt with; how one becomes a member of the group (for example, the price of admission is tears); how consensus is assessed (for example, by silence); what kind of feedback will be acceptable (only positive, only brutal, and so forth); how to deal with disagreements, conflicts, and so forth. The trainer's influence can be crucial (Psathas and Hardert, 1966): by his interventions he selects those interactions which will be focused upon and thereby are called important. These should be dealt with openly as part of handling the authority question and particularly the trainer. One important norm would be that norms ought to be explicit and that everyone have the opportunity to react to each norm.

There are many ways to look at the growth of a group (although the data are certainly not clear cut to show that groups do go through stages which can be identified to establish the stage of growth). Nevertheless, these are useful ways of thinking about the life of a group and may help generate other ideas as well. The work of Bion and others (Bion, 1961; Stock and Thelen, 1958) has led to the formulation of a theory that identifies and classifies two parts of participant interaction within group development as the work level (how much) and the emotional climate. The latter is categorized into themes (fight, flight, pairing, counterpairing, dependency, and counterdependency). This is a cyclical theory in which problems recur and must be resolved over and over again. A modified cyclical theory is the well-developed one of Bennis and Shepard (1956). As they point out, individuals—in their usual groups— have already worked out their relations with both authority and their peers, relationships often imposed by any particular system: for example, parent-children, teacher-students, and employer-employees. In a T-group, all the usual requirements are absent, and participants have the opportunity to experience once again how they feel about these important questions as they go about making a temporary society and observing how they establish their relationships. Whatever they do becomes data.

Much emotion is attached to the resultant interactions; these reactions should be examined by the participants as well as the solutions arrived at. Like Freud, Bennis and Shepard say that the members must first deal with the authority figure and then with other members. When they are freed from dealing with the leader (if they are not overly dependent or counterdependent), they can turn to each other. In time, members can acknowledge that the group is important without overpersonal or counterpersonal behavior interfering. By then members can appreciate each other's differences and see each as an individual not as a member of a class or as someone playing a role: Mary, not "the woman;" John, not "the minister," and so forth. If this is worked out, then interpersonal disagreements should be around issues instead of around hidden emotional personal agenda items. Thus members can deal with what is said rather than who said it.

Individuals progress at different stages as the group develops. Nevertheless, it does help to think about groups developing as a frame of reference when sorting out what is happening. As laboratories are being designed more and more for "family" groups, they can effect more extended group growth and development. As the stages develop, communication presumably becomes clearer and less distorted. Whether or not the changes will be taken away and used depends on how well the individual has integrated these new learnings, and what his back-home situation will permit. The group needs at least some members with little conflict about the problem of a particular phase: for example, dependence or authority and/ or interdependence with peers. Such people are called *catalysts,* and the actions they take which allow the group to move on are called *barometric events* (Bennis and Shepard, 1956). Meanwhile, uninterrupted focus on the here-and-now and immediate feedback are always imperative, allowing all participants to share in the experience and to have data to compare with their own perceptions and interpretations. If someone who is counterdependent continues to see the trainer as manipulative and making all the decisions although he is not, this can be checked against other participants' perceptions. If someone thinks that everyone must like everyone else and that there can be no disagreements, then he can learn that another member finds it quite comfortable to differentiate his feelings toward various members, and indeed, disagrees heartily with several on a number of issues. Obviously, it is necessary to have a

variety of people and it is unlikely the group can make much progress if by chance most of the members should be conflicted about
dependency, for example; indeed, we would then be in a therapy
group. If at least the authority issue has been resolved, participants
can appreciate each other as possible resources for help, thus enab-
ling them to make "contract" arrangements with particular individuals so that they can act as consultants to each other on back-home
problems. Moreover, they can agree to oversee each other (even if
from a long distance) to insure that these commitments are pursued.

In addition to such cyclical theories, there are also developmental theories that see groups progressing through stages, for
example, forming, storming, norming, and performing (Tuckman,
1965). There also are life-cycle theories which describe groups as
going through birth, development, and death, analogous to the life
of an individual (Mann, 1967; Mills, 1964; Slater, 1966).

As mentioned earlier, it is unlikely that many time-limited
groups reach complete maturity. Still it may be helpful, as Dimock
(1970) says, to picture an ideal group in terms of the four dimensions of Gibb's theory of trust formation (1964b), another frame
of reference for looking at group development, to know what it
might be like when trust is well established:

> *Acceptance:* There is a high degree of acceptance among
> members with little fear or distrust. There is a genuine warmth
> with few attempts at artificial small talk or humor. "Odd
> ball" members are accepted and individual differences are en-
> couraged. There is a lot of confidence in the group and little
> need to be compared with other groups.
> *Data flow.* Members listen to one another and share
> information. Decisions are made on the basis of information
> available, including outside resources, with all members par-
> ticipating. Members express their real feelings and use the
> reactions of others to these feelings in adjusting their behavior.
> *Goal processing.* The interests and goals of members
> are resolved and integrated into a common purpose. In iden-
> tifying with a common purpose members show enthusiastic,
> purposeful, creative work. The group can change its goals as
> they accomplish one task and move on to the next. Members
> learn and grow as the group engages in a variety of activities

suitable to their goals. There is no need for outside stimulation or rewards.

Control. Organization is flexible and is set up on terms of the goals of the group. Leadership is shared as the group-building and task roles are widely distributed among group members. The power structure is open and varies in response to needs and resources. Formal methods of operating are not necessary. Members are able to reject group standards and still be part of the group as feelings and conflicts are openly expressed (Dimock, 1970, p. 15).

Schein (1969, p. 62) developed a simple but helpful self-rating questionnaire which members can fill out several times in the course of a group experience. It can provide another useful way of looking at group growth and development and can be used to focus on areas for future growth, or to evaluate growth which has been achieved (see Table 9).

Leadership and Authority

As we have seen, the help-sharing model which involves collaboration and shared leadership moves the group towards self-management. Leadership and authority are distributed, and individuals learn to share the responsibility for providing the leadership functions which are required at different times during the life of the group. Members come to be seen as resources and are valued for their differences. The trainer is seen as a unique member but then so too is each other member, in his own way. Among the participants, there may, theoretically at least, be all the skills, knowledge, and ability to make appropriate interventions that are required for the work and maintenance of the group.

The T-group is, of course, training in shared leadership based on the democratic ethic. It will be recalled that the early proponents of the laboratory method were concerned that individuals in this technologically advanced and bureaucratized world would not be able to be or feel effective. They believed that the quality of participation determines whether any particular human democratic process will succeed or fail and that training is the key to whether or not there is high quality in participative actions.

Table 9. CRITERIA OF GROUP MATURITY

1. Adequate mechanisms for getting feedback

| Poor feedback mechanisms | 1   2   3   4   5 Average | Excellent feedback mechanisms |

2. Adequate decision making procedure

| Poor decision making procedure | 1   2   3   4   5 Average | Very adequate decision making |

3. Optimal cohesion

| Low cohesion | 1   2   3   4   5 Average | Optimal cohesion |

4. Flexible organization and procedures

| Very inflexible | 1   2   3   4   5 Average | Very flexible |

5. Maximum use of member resources

| Poor use of resources | 1   2   3   4   5 Average | Excellent use of resources |

6. Clear communications

| Poor communications | 1   2   3   4   5 Average | Excellent communications |

7. Clear goals accepted by members

| Unclear goals— not accepted | 1   2   3   4   5 Average | Very clear goals— accepted |

8. Feelings of interdependence with authority persons

| No interdependence | 1   2   3   4   5 Average | High interdependence |

9. Shared participation in leadership functions

| Not shared participation | 1   2   3   4   5 Average | High shared participation |

10. Acceptance of minority views and persons

| No acceptance | 1   2   3   4   5 Average | High acceptance |

SOURCE: Edgar H. Schein, *Process Consultation: Its Role in Organization Development* (Menlo Park, Calif.: Addison-Wesley, 1969), p. 62

Autocratic leadership takes on responsibility for all functions, task and maintenance. In the T-group, the trainer may model functional leadership (that is, carry out a particular function when it is required, for example, clarify or encourage, summarize or harmonize), or he may point out the absent role through an intervention and leave it for other members to fill the need, until these needs have become clearer to the participants themselves. The variety of interventions, in addition to his personal behavior, which a trainer uses as he shares himself and his skills, has been well described in an article by Dyer (1969). These include: content focus, process focus, asking for feelings, direction-giving (which in some ways correspond to Luft's [1969] structural interventions), direct feedback, cognitive orientations, performing task and maintenance functions (and perhaps even some dysfunctional behaviors which satisfy his own personal needs such as recognition-seeking), diagnostic intervention, and protection intervention. Dyer goes on to suggest that there should be more research in this area about the relationship of, for example, kinds of interventions and learning outcomes for participants. He also suggests that an inventory of interventions be assembled which might be helpful in implementing particular outcomes.

It is important to remember here that, theoretically, all of these interventions are available for the use of participants so that all can become "expert" members and influence the group's direction. It does not mean to imply that one T-group experience equips a participant for the work of being a trainer; rather, the experience equips him or her for more effective membership in democratic groups with shared leadership.

Intergroup Processes

The laboratory method is a way of looking at one's usual behavior and its impact on others; it is also an opportunity to try other ways of interacting and looking at the consequences. Over the years, a variety of exercises have been designed that allow groups to understand what happens between groups under various conditions. Originally an exercise was developed by Blake and others (1964) that arranges the conditions for two groups to compete in the design of a product. Representatives of each then try to negotiate for whose product is better, fail, and turn the decision over to judges. The data collected illustrate that each group overvalues its own representatives and considers the other group's representatives as irrational and unfair. Also, the losing group makes scapegoats of its own representatives. Often, however, participants feel they have been manipulated into the competition.

Harrison (1969), believing the more usual everyday situation makes possible competition *or* collaboration, designed an exercise to demonstrate that given the opportunity to do either, groups usually compete. This design eliminates being able to blame the staff; thus participants come to recognize that they are likely to compete in a competition-collaboration situation. In a given situation, each group designs a product to the same specifications and then representatives meet to find a joint product using the separate contributions. If they cannot agree, then staff help with the suggestions about how to problem-solve collaboratively, allowing practice in collaboration. Again, overwhelmingly the groups rate their own product as higher and see their own negotiators as more collaborative and fairer.

One important learning here is practice with collaboration as suggested by the staff, for example: "In a second negotiation session, each negotiator is given an observer from his own group who is responsible for intervening and to point out competitive behavior on his part and collaborative moves on the part of the other group's negotiators" (Harrison, 1969, p. 54). As Harrison says (quoting Morton Deutsch): "Interventions which are designed to increase collaboration and reduce competitive behavior should produce positive changes in one or more of the following directions: (1) an increase in willingness to collaborate or the setting of norms of collaborative behavior; (2) an understanding that the frustrations, hostilities, and distorted perceptions arising during the negotiations are connected to the competitive orientation, (3) a perception that the negotiating situation has changed in such a way as to facilitate collaboration and inhibit competition; (4) an increase in the perceived gain to come from collaboration and decrease in the perceived likelihood of gain from an orientation to compete and win" (Harrison, 1969, p. 55).

This demonstration of how to overcome competition through collaboration is a learning which participants can take back home. Obviously lessons in collaboration are necessary since it seldom occurs spontaneously.

Place of Conceptualization

Paralleling the experiential part of the T-group is some activity related to understanding what is going on. One problem to be avoided is oversimplification: that is, to concentrate some theoretical notions into a twenty-minute presentation often leads to some loss of appreciation for the complexities of understanding human behavior. However, these can provide frames of reference for trying to understand the meanginfulness of human interaction, and they may lead the participant to explore the theory further.

Some commonly used short lectures have been printed in various places, particularly in the handbooks issued by NTL (1969, 1970c, 1970d). These are related to such topics as personality organization, styles of leadership, planned change, force field analysis, how to observe in groups, conflict resolutions, and resistance to change. They are often presented in the large general meeting when it seems appropriate for the learning of several T-groups which are meeting simultaneously. In addition, there are skill exercises—such as listening, identifying leadership roles, role playing, and nonverbal exercises—for focusing on a learning that is better highlighted in that manner (Pfeiffer and Jones, 1969). Intergroup exercises are commonly held in laboratories in order to bring the subjects to the participants' attention. They also give them the opportunity to experience the emotional involvement elicited by competition and collaboration.

In these cases, data collecting and evaluation are built in and discussed to give participants some appreciation for the method of inquiry as an integral part of the laboratory method. How the trainers feel about these experiences will very much influence the attitudes of the participants. Such activities are intended to engage the intellect, but they all evoke emotional correlates which also need to be acknowledged and dealt with.

Trainers and Co-trainers

Although the discussion in this chapter has referred to a singular trainer, it is important to comment briefly on who the trainers are, what kinds of cotrainers have been used traditionally, and why the relationship between cotrainers is important for the group.

Not only are individual trainers role models; the relationship between trainers is a demonstration of interpersonal relatedness and effectiveness. Traditionally the trainer has been a white male. This situation has been changing slowly but intentionally. In some places (for example, training programs at the University of Massachusetts) a heterosexual pair of trainers is the model which is intentionally used as often as possible, and interracial pairs are used if possible. This is an important issue, for sexism and racism must be confronted among trainers as well as in the group.

Little research has been published on the nature of the cotraining relationship or on its effects on training outcomes. This very important area is well worth much attention and research. A recent contribution to it, although primarily directed to psychoanalytically oriented therapy groups, raises many issues relevant to cotrainers as well: "The question is not whether or not there will be issues between therapists regarding sex roles, race, timing of interventions, competition, or anything else, for these are the sum and substance of cotherapist interaction. What is important is the *quality* of the interaction: how much basic openness and willingness to communicate is present as balanced against the degree of antagonism and distrust" (F. B. Davis and Lohr, 1971, p. 157).

Transfer of Learnings

Participants who come to T-groups by and large are already effective members of other groups. And they should not go away less effective than they were when they came, which means that the learnings of the training experience should be integrated before the group ends. In part, this means setting learning goals that can be reached in the time available. It also means conscious planning for transfer before the group ends, for example, through consultation with other participants and other resource members of the learning community. The participant needs to make his own plans for this transfer as well as for learning goals during training. It would be helpful if these learning goals could be combined into "contract arrangements" with at least one other participant to enable some real carry-over from the here-and-now to the there-and-then. Learning how to use resources and to collaborate with peers is certainly one of the intentions of this experience and can be built into the design to be taken away.

A less useful way of dealing with this novel experience of a T-group would be to encapsulate it and see it as very special but without relation to the real world. Equally unfortunate would be a decision to try to reproduce the whole experience outside without taking into account that the situation back home cannot be immediately accommodated to the alternative way of working and relating in a T-group. Planning for changes could mean doing a force field analysis of what the back-home situation is like and learning how to decrease restraining forces so that changes can be made. This does place a good deal of emphasis on intentionality and conceptualization which the design of the laboratory must take into account. If most of the time is spent on the unique part of the total experience—that is, learning to be in touch with one's feelings and to communicate about this learning experience and recognizing that others are also dealing with personal perceptions of common events which may differ; knowing that there are hidden agenda items as well as the task at hand; and being aware that many decisions are made implicitly, not explicitly—then, although all are important learnings, the learnings which would make it possible to utilize these experiences productively afterwards may be neglected. How to take away what is learned needs to be an integral part of the experience.

Extensions

Largely we have been dealing with the typical *stranger group* which has, in the past, involved working for a short period of time (typically a weekend to two-weeks) in an isolated setting where there is no carryover in relationships from the workshop to the back-home situation. However, there is a growing trend to work with nonstranger groups where the learnings can be transferred more directly. These have been called *family groups* (all of the people are "related" in some way, for example, they work in the same department or live in the same dormitory). Obviously openness and risk-taking are limited in the beginning as people think about changing over from a traditional, competitive, nonexposing environment to a collaborative, authentic environment. There will need to be a recognition that change takes place over time and attitudes do not change overnight. Change programs should be framed in terms of years, not days, if we are to consider changing large systems; certainly in terms of at least months, if we are talking of an academic year.

Whether or not the change agents are from inside the organization or are outside consultants is also important. However, not only formal organizations will want to work with consultant change agents. Many "temporary" systems which will increase in number will find it important to think about maintenance as well as task as members try to work together, or live together. An example that brings this point home very clearly is an experiment in off-campus living-learning which some students organized:

A group of students arranged for independent study credit for a spring semester and went to live in a single house on a small island off the coast of Massachusetts. Their intentions were to be useful to each other intellectually as well as interpersonally, and they went through a formalized selection and somewhat less formalized orientation process over a period of several weeks. They kept diaries of their experience during the semester for a course they were all taking as part of this planned experience; and they attempted to process their experiences, both without and with the occasional help of outside consultants.

What is relevant to note here is that their original intention was to have a group facilitator live with them. The plan did not materialize, but in evaluating the experience it was very clear that a regular consultant would have been a very important addition both during the orientation period and during the semester. It would also have been useful to have a built-in, formally acknowledged termination with evaluation, again with a process consultant.

If alternatives for living/learning/working groups are to have a better chance of meeting the expectations and intentions (often unclear and implicit) of the participants, then laboratory educators, change agents, group facilitators will be more and more called on as resource people [Appley and Clark, 1971].

We have seen earlier that theory can serve to help researcher, trainer, and participant select, understand, and make sense out of what is going on. For the researcher, however, there are many difficult problems in an applied behavioral science. Still the whole renewed interest in action research (Sanford, 1970; M. B. Smith, 1969) would seem to confirm that it is timely and important for behavioral science and social action to combine forces, and training laboratories will be an important place for such research efforts. Trainers must feel some reciprocal responsibility with theorists and researchers; if what is central in training is a spirit of inquiry, then indeed all trainers need to be aware of, and related to, research and theory. Indeed participants, too, need to become partners in research.

There are, of course, many difficult design and methodology problems in evaluating T-group and laboratory effectiveness and in testing related theories. Some behavioral scientists are working on these problems, including House (1967a), whose contribution to the methodology of evaluation is summarized by Buchanan (1969, p. 466): "House (1967a) classified the variables relevant to the problem of evaluation into four categories: objectives of the training, initial states of the learner, initial states of the organization, and methods of inducing change in the learner. Then, considering the methods as *input* variables, the objectives of the laboratory training as *output* variables, and the initial states of both the participants and the organization as *moderators,* he generated a paradigm of relationships that highlighted the issues in planning and assessing organizational development efforts and outlined a specific assessment design to illustrate the paradigm."

Complementing this attempt to deal with *general* problems of design is Harrison (1968), who has tried to present a thorough analysis of *specific* issues. Although he reviews the problems that researchers are likely to be confronted with, he has written for the "consumers" as well as the "creators" of research, recognizing that important practical decisions are being made by administrators and practitioners about training projects. His monograph is as lucid in style as it is critically analytic, and it should fulfill his intention to stimulate others to attack the problems to which solutions may be in the offing, and also to encourage others to be courageous in the face of uncertainty and lack of elegant tools.

Having reminded us that it has always been difficult to measure learning processes and outcomes, and even more so when dealing with such concepts as interpersonal behavior, Harrison discusses three important issues: controls, temporal change in training outcome, and dimensions and direction of change. In the first case, the problem of controls, he points out that the very act of putting some people into a training group and others into a control group already biases the outcomes for each participant and those with whom he interacts. Also, selection for training often takes place before the program and cannot be resolved by random assignment. Nor is it feasible often to use delayed assignments, with some volunteers taking their training at a later date. So a valid and practical solution is to study the *process* of training as well as the *outcomes,* which means that, where possible, all are given training but perhaps using different depth of personal involvement, for example, lectures, case studies, and T-groups; or different lengths of training. Then we can look for differential outcomes. "The assumption behind these designs is that if the amount and kind of training outcome vary systematically and predictably as functions of some input (whether the design, the type of participant, the behavior of training staff, or whatever), then the obtained changes can be viewed as "real": Because all groups being compared have been through a training experience, the design eliminates the biasing of perception which occurs when an untrained control group is used" (Harrison, 1968, p. 12).

A variation of this effort to evaluate training is to look at some behavior(s) of the participants during training, and predict post-training behavior on the basis of those independent process variables (for example, active involvement in training and changes in interpersonal perception after training). Thus the problems of control can begin to be met creatively and meaningfully.

The second problem, temporal change in training outcome, is raised as a reminder that we talk about longitudinal changes but rarely follow up on participants over time. Harrison goes on to make a strong case for giving changes time to occur and be stabilized (perhaps six months or more) rather than measuring changes only before and immediately after the laboratory. He supports this point of view theoretically, as, for example, by referring it to the Schein and Bennis three-stage temporal theory of change (1965). This theory was originally conceptualized by Lewin (1947) and included *unfreezing* as the first stage of learning, that is, preparing to learn by having some disconfirmation of an attitude about oneself through feedback. (See also Nadler, 1969.) Time is necessary for the new behavior to be tried and tested and then be integrated conceptually and experientially so that a new state of quasi-equilibrium is gained. To measure outcomes would (or should) mean to measure this *new* state, but we have not been able to observe how long this process takes. Although such measurement does require invention of instruments and methods, it is obviously important to explore. Some studies have indeed shown increased changes in behavior with the passage of time.

Harrison also raises the question of what changes to measure and whether we will acknowledge *any* change as change. This problem requires at least some consideration as we look at outcomes. In any case, we implicitly say what we value by what we measure, so it is well to be explicit. He also describes a classification system for training outcomes, pointing out that many researches are normative: for example, it is considered good to become democratic, and bad to become authoritarian. Normative outcomes are often desired by researchers, clients, and companies, as opposed to "it-depends-on-what-the-individual-needs-to-do" kind of outcomes. Practitioners studying outcomes often are concerned with *individual change* as the desired outcome. However, in one extreme, all the individual differences could get rubbed off or changed, and people would become more alike if normative outcomes are the goal. More happily, each person could be encouraged to develop the underdeveloped parts of himself that he wishes to develop.

Harrison urges that methods be developed for studying what may be the most important goals of laboratory training in human relations: the development of adaptive and learning capacity. This is still a third position which he points out and, although theoretically very important, it is almost never used. It is based on Bennis's goals of laboratory training, discussed earlier. Finally, Harrison deplores the *cult of originality* which means that trainers continue inventing designs when actually we "do not even know enough theoretically about the effects of different elements of training design even to permit us to classify laboratories according to design" (Harrison, 1968, p. 17).

Many questions remain to be answered. These need to be formulated first, then tested. As Argyris points out, with new variables to understand, we need to phrase new kinds of questions to find the answers we are looking for, and we must create settings in which these variables may exist. As he suggests, "we have arrived at the point where applied behavioral science can be central to basic research in the social psychology of interpersonal relations" (Argyris, 1969, p. 907). Furthermore, as Harrison (1968), and Rogers (1970), and others have suggested, we shall have to take participants in as partners in research; we will want to use naturalistic observation and natural settings as well as to work out of artificial T-groups and laboratories.

We could, of course, go on wishing for a giant theorist-methodologist to bring more order to the field; meanwhile, we must accept the shared leadership method of collaboration as we formulate questions and try to be imaginative about searching for answers.

We have examined the human relations laboratory orientation as one available way people today can take time out from their routinized and familiar, role-related group memberships to experiment with alternative ways of living and working together with other people. We have tried to demonstrate the importance of creating a learning environment which makes this possible and have explored the ways in which special resource people (called trainers) are critically important in this quasi-controlled environment. We also have tried to show that members must be able and willing to interact freely in order for laboratory training to be possible; therefore, we confronted the question of who the participants shall be and examined the requirements as well as the opportunities for participation. How a group develops and what processes go on in groups were explored by examining some group protocols and several theoretical formulations. Finally, some directions for research were explored, and some implications for integration of theory, research, and practice were discussed.

Chapter V

≋≋≋≋≋≋

Issues and Procedures in Training Group Therapists

A book whose subject matter is group process is, in effect, a book on training and is written to familiarize the student with and instruct him in that field. A book, however, is not a substitute for a training program. Reading about practice can only partially acquaint the student with some of the issues involved in becoming a practitioner, and for this reason we dedicate a separate chapter to training. For those who wish to practice group psychotherapy, an understanding of the issues in training is important for several reasons. First, since therapy deals with the uniqueness of the human being, the most complex of all systems, it has never established either its basic assumptions or its techniques with anything like finality. Second, since group therapy has recently become popular as a means of therapeutic intervention, both the need and the demand for group therapists have rapidly increased. This development has required that certain assumptions about training have to be reexamined in light of the need to create a greater supply of practitioners. Third, many practitioners are recruited from the areas of individual therapy, counseling, and casework, with the thought that they will transfer their skills in one-to-one relationships to the group setting. These practitioners, however, soon realize that they are dealing with an entirely different theraputic milieu for which they are unprepared.

The first issue in group therapy education is the selection and recruitment of students. In 1967 there were seventeen programs for group psychotherapists, ranging all the way from modest programs in relatively rural areas to programs in prestigious psychiatic training centers in highly psychiatrically sophisticated urban complexes. (The executive secretary of AGPA told us in June 1973 that the Standards and Ethics Committee hopes to have a new list by 1974.) While we have not been able to obtain standards for admission to all these programs, a few examples demonstrate current thinking about admission requirements. The Dallas Group Psychotherapy Society (1965) states: "Trainees will be psychiatrists, clinical psychologists, and psychiatric social workers. Prerequisite for psychiatrists will be completion of a three-year residency in psychiatry. For clinical psychologists, the prerequisite will be state certification as a psychologist. For social workers, the prerequisite will be a master's degree in social work and membership in the Academy of Certified Social Workers."

The New York School of Psychiatry informs us in personal correspondence (1967) that "all the students are psychiatric residents." A considerably broader definition of participants is included in the Group Work Training Program of Saint Elizabeth's Hospital in Washington, D.C. (1966):

Interns and residents in psychiatry, psychology, psychodrama, and the chaplaincy attend upon recommendation of their training supervisors. Staff members in the prevailing array of mental health disciplines attend upon administrative approval of their supervisor and upon an eligibility determination by the Admissions Committee, a subcommittee of the Group Work Advisory Committee. Each applicant is evaluated in terms of personal aptitude, educational background, and relevant experience. Educational requirements include a minimum of a bachelor's degree with courses leading to an understanding of sociological and psychological principles and/or satisfactory completion of preparatory training in group work, as required by the discipline. Experience and personal requirements include demonstration of perceptiveness, articulateness, potential for independent action, commitment to group methods of treatment, and applicant's ability to conceptualize psychodynamics consistent with his professional training and experience.

The American Group Psychotherapy Association (AGPA) Standards and Ethics Committee in its 1966 report states flatly that "group therapists are qualified mental health professionals committed to the practice of group psychotherapy." The use of the inclusive term *mental health professional* suggests that the association was calling for a more liberal policy of selection of candidates for training than had previously been reflected in admission requirements of the various educational centers.

More recently the AGPA (1968) points to a more exclusive concept of who should be trained. They state that the minimal prerequisite of professional and educational experience to qualify as a candidate is as follows: for psychiatrists, the M.D. degree and one year of approved psychiatric residency; for clinical psychologists, a Ph.D. degree in clinical psychology or the equivalent, or state certification as a clinical psychologist; for social workers, a M.S.W. degree and two years of qualified, supervised experience in a psychiatric agency or clinic. "Candidates in any of these categories must have completed at least two hundred hours doing individual psychotherapy under qualified supervision, with psychiatrists, psychologists, and social workers participating as a team, before entering the group psychotherapy training program."

Unfortunately, the conservative trend of the AGPA guidelines can result only in a relatively small number of adequately trained professionals entering the field. The increasing demand for group therapists is presently being met in large part by individuals who are not in the mental health professions (and thus are limited in their preparation for the job) and whose training is sometimes limited to a few group experiences as participants. One becomes concerned that the AGPA, in tightly controlling the requirements for admission to training for group psychotherapy, will end up in the same position as the medical field with an acute shortage of practitioners to meet a growing public demand.

We take the position that this problem can best be solved by liberalizing training program entrance requirements. The 1966 guidelines were a step in the right direction, and they should be further extended to include candidates from all the helping professions. The heavy reliance in the 1968 statement on academic preparation of the candidates is certainly questionable. Academic success is not necessarily correlated with the personal skills that contribute to success as a therapist. In fact, our own observations are that these traits that predispose toward academic excellence (such as objectivity and critical judgment) are developed at the expense of personal warmth and empathy. In addition, the acceptance of the scientific model, so much a part of graduate work in the behavioral sciences, may result in the candidate's accepting this model as his philosophy of help-giving. He then frequently perceives help-giving as manipulative and the client as dehumanized. In order to ensure good practice, the primary factors in selection should be the personal qualities of the applicant, the applicant's help-giving philosophy, and his academic preparation, in that order.

A second issue in group psychotherapy education is whether the help-giving model the student brings to the training program can be transferred to the group therapy relationship. This is a major issue in training, for if the therapist has not clearly related his model of help-giving to his personal style, his style may interfere with his therapeutic judgment. His attitude toward the group members which serves to reduce his anxiety when confronted with the group may be authoritarian, seductive, or defensive. In any case, these attitudes can act against the interest of the group members. When the student comes from the mental health professions, as is currently the practice, his help-giving model most likely conforms to the medical model. The help receiver in this model is usually called a patient and is presumed to be sick and in need of therapeutic intervention on the part of the helper. The helper in turn is in the generic role of a therapist, which calls for him to assume a degree of expertness and authority; it also places limits on him in terms of how equal, intimate, personally involved, and emotionally expressive he may be.

Traditional and psychoanalytic group psychotherapists favor supporting and integrating this definition of the helper role into the role of a group therapist. Experiential group therapists, especially those who practice the encounter method, have largely increased their method of personal involvement and self-expression in the group setting. They nevertheless continue to contain their increased emotional expressiveness within the role of expert, for the doctor still knows best when to "lay on hands" and for what purposes.

Those engaged in conducting group treatment generally assume that there is a dimension to working with a group that is not present in the dyadic relationship. This assumption is based upon their observations of certain behaviors that occur when a small number of people meet together in a face-to-face relationship. These behaviors and how to use them for therapeutic effect should be understood by the group therapist in training. One of these behaviors is the pressure the group exerts toward conformity among members about what constitutes reality in the group, that is, what beliefs, feelings, and actions are acceptable and appropriate for members to hold and pursue and what beliefs and emotions are inappropriate and should be dropped by either patient or therapist. Much experimental work has verified that the pressure toward conformity is a powerful dimension of small group behavior.

The group also has a great capacity to establish shared norms of behavior and to impose them on its members. The therapist must be ready to challenge those norms that are destructive to the therapeutic process and to support and further norms that advance this process.

In addition, the group can function quite effectively to support resistance to change. Members frequently seek roles that are consistent both with their characterological defenses and with the group's wish to resist therapeutic progress. The help-rejecting complainer is likely to find his masochistic approach to interpersonal relations fully supported by his fellow patients, while "the doctor's assistant" may find encouragement from group members who find his upstaging of the therapist to their defensive advantage. Scapegoating can occur in this context and is an even greater danger to the group therapeutic process. The therapist must be aware of the collusion between group members in setting up these resistive roles. He must prepare to intervene therapeutically, to confront, to interpret, and to suggest alternative behavior.

Another aspect of small groups is the opportunity they offer for multiple transferences to occur. Group members may appear to other members not as they really are but as transference figures who serve as suitable objects for the working through of previously unresolved relationships with people from the member's background. One patient may behave toward another as he previously has to a spouse, a younger sibling, a favorite uncle. These transferences may reflect relatively recent experiences or those of early childhood. This behavior may lead to perceptions of the others that are obviously not in keeping with their role in the group. The therapist must be alert to help the patient work toward a resolution of these transferences with the aid of the group.

Finally, the therapist must come to realize that the group can greatly magnify the individual's feeling of anxiety. This is especially true in initial sessions, when the patient is faced with anxiety over self-revelation and with the possibility of the group's responding with ridicule, criticism, or rejection. The therapist must understand the intensity of this anxiety and know how to alleviate it by building a sense of trust among the members and between the members and himself.

In addition to the knowledge the student needs to have about the group, he must have knowledge about himself. He must not only be aware of the dimensions of group behavior, he must also be perceptive and sensitive to the individuals who compose the group. He must empathize with each if these persons at all times in the group if he is to make responsible therapeutic interventions. He must, for example, be aware of how the patient feels when he assumes certain anxiety-producing roles. How does the patient feel when he is very assertive or when he is most passive? How does he feel when he reveals intimate details of his personal relationships? What experience is the patient undergoing when he is under attack by others in the group or when his belief in himself is questioned? Should the therapist lack empathy, he may thoughtlessly intervene in a way that exposes the patient to unnecessary and untherapeutic anxiety or he may neglect to intervene when the patient needs his warmth and support to survive and grow in the group setting.

The student also needs to be aware of how his personal style affects his role as a therapist. To the extent the therapist is unaware of his personal style, he attempts to fashion the role of helper to reduce his anxiety. Of the many personal styles the therapist can adopt to achieve this reduction of anxiety, most are at the expense of the personal growth of group members. He may appear as a powerful and central figure, or he may be intimate and seductive, or he may be cold and distant. He may selectively encourage certain types of discussion while effectively turning off other behaviors. Most damaging of all, he may manipulate other group members by placing them in the service of his defensive style so that they are no longer free agents seeking to grow through a therapeutic experience but bondsmen in the service of a tyrant. Most training programs pay too little attention to showing a student how his personal style may subvert the therapeutic role. Although those who run such programs are aware of the need to recognize, modify, and control those personal needs of a trainee which can lead him to establish a role for himself that works against the therapeutic process, they tend to expect the supervisor to work on this problem with the student. Some movement toward increased acceptance of this aspect of training can be observed in the 1968 AGPA guideline to group therapy training centers, which strongly recommends a personal psychotherapeutic experience. The addition of this experience to a training program shows that some trainers now recognize that supervision is not a substitute for psychotherapy and that the neophyte therapist can profit by the understanding of his personality acquired through his participation in the training program.

A third issue in training is what the student needs to know

about how patients are helped in a therapy group. There is, as yet, no single theory of group psychotherapy that satisfactorily answers this question. Some training programs tend to be selective with respect to both theories and contributors to a single theory. Some programs prefer to be eclectic in their approach. They base this eclecticism on the philosophy that if the trainee is exposed to a number of theoretical ideas, he can, in practice, test for himself which ideas help him understand what happens in the group and what interventions can be successfully applied to achieve therapeutic results. Our experience is that this philosophy, while it may be sound in the area of politics, is not always educationally sound. We suggest that a single well-defined approach be followed by the student. Once he has successfully mastered this theory of group psychotherapy and can translate his understandings of the concepts into practice, he is free to enlarge his theoretical background and either choose from among several theories or become as electic as he wishes. In the integrating process, the student must combine his theoretical understanding of the members' psychodynamics with his empathy for the members and his own psychic reactions in a manner that permits him to effectively move the group toward a successful resolution of the conflicts of each member. To accomplish this task he will have had to have previous instruction and experience in the techniques of timing and expression so that he is able to apply his interventions in the immediate situation and so that he is able to utilize group feedback to critically judge the success or failure of those interventions.

Now that we have presented some of the issues involved in group therapy education and some of the difficulties and complexities involved in resolving those issues, we discuss here some of the procedures and programs that address themselves to these issues. The specific question asked by educators in the field is "What procedures will provide adequate learning?" While we are unable to find a single procedure that is used by a great number of programs, the majority rely upon a combination of didactic learning and supervision.

Programs in didactic learning usually are modeled upon the course structure commonly used in academic institutions, especially (but by no means limited to) training programs conducted under the aegis of academic institutions. Most such courses, therefore, are conducted within a semester time unit and utilize lectures, assigned readings, and, in a few cases, a final examination. The proponents of didactic learning argue that this approach provides students with a systematic exposure to the theories and concepts in the field with the result that the student understands how the group acts as a therapeutic agent, how people are helped in a group, and the relationship of personal dynamics to group behavior. A major disadvantage of this approach is the attitude toward the subject matter that it fosters in the student. Group therapy is not an academic field to be mastered by amassing information through intellectualizing; rather, it involves an awareness of interpersonal relationships that requires sensitivity, intimacy, and willingness to relate warmly to others. Thus the instructor should remember that the course is in understanding human interaction, not chemistry or experimental psychology, and that the student should come to approach the subject matter personally rather than intellectually. (See Mullan and Rosenbaum, 1962, for a reading list on this subject.)

The instructor can introduce a personal dimension into a didactic course in two ways. One involves timing: for example, the course may be presented after the student has had some experience as an observer or as a group participant. A second involves combining teaching methods that are both participative and didactic. The student can be required to participate in role-playing and human relations exercises, which can be interspersed with lectures and readings. Or he can be exposed to groups through the use of audiovisual materials, notably tapes and films.

Because participative learning methods are coming into increasingly greater use in many training programs, we discuss some of their uses here. The most traditional of these methods is the student's contact with groups through tapes, films, or the observation of live groups. The major advantage of tapes and films is that they can simulate the live experience and therefore heighten student involvement. Students tend to identify with the group members and the therapist, thereby permitting discussion of the student's level of empathy for patients and understanding of what is occurring in the group. This method is especially useful also in studying the effect of therapeutic interventions and the resultant feedback that informs the therapist of the group's acceptance or rejection of his interventions. This procedure is well suited to accomplish these results because tapes and films can be stopped and, if necessary, played over and over again. The major disadvantage of using tapes and films is that they are not the "real thing," and the student is unable to respond to the material as if he were present, either as a group member or as a cotherapist. Observing live groups is a transitional experience between tapes and video presentations and actually participating as a group member or a group therapist, which is the most effective kind of participative learning. Group observation is most successful if the student observes from behind a one-way screen with an audio system. Observation in the same room as the group does not permit the observer to discuss the group interactions while they are in process. He must also be constantly aware of his role as observer so that he is not caught up in the tensions of the group and so that he does not lose control of his own reactions and distract the group members. The therapist, in either situation, should be available to the students so that they can check their feeling for the group experience with him, and so that they can compare his intuitions on the nature of the group communications and the impact of the therapist's interventions with their own observations.

Role-playing and human relations training exercises are forms of participative learning. Role-playing gives the student the opportunity to see a situation as another would see it and to assume the responsibility for behaving as the other person would behave. A typical use of role-playing is to have a group of students role-play a therapy group, with members rotating in the role of the therapist. Afterward, the students talk over what has occurred in the group, what has been conveyed by the group and individual communication, and how the therapist handled the experience. The advantage to the students is that they can get the feeling for both therapist and patient roles before running a "live" group.

Human relations training exercises run the gamut from simple sensory awareness exercises involving touching and eye contact to fairly elaborate designs developed to train T-group facilitators in complex techniques of group management. Students who come to a group therapy training program with previous experience in the development of trust, openness of communication, and contact with their own feelings can readily dispense with these simple exercises. Those students, however, and they may be in the majority, who come out of highly organized graduate programs which emphasize cognitive learning may not have developed these interpersonal skills. All too often in the field, a highly developed cognitive style is assumed to coexist with highly developed interpersonal skills. The caveat here is that if the students are lacking these skills, the training program should be prepared to provide them. Complex human relations designs can provide the student with skills he will need as a therapist. For example, we have prepared a design to precede the student's experience as a cotherapist in a "live" group. The exercise places an emphasis on the learning of shared communication; the nine steps take approximately an hour and twenty-five minutes: (1) Introductory remarks help to create an atmosphere for the session and shut out the members' preceding experiences and commitments. Two to three minutes. (2) A self-confrontation centers around a particular problem set for the group. This step involves a period of introspective silence. Five minutes. (3) Cotrainer dyads share personal reflections on the problem under consideration. Ten minutes. (4) A pair of dyads combines and all four members share their personal reflections on the problem under consideration. Ten minutes. (5) The four member groups break up into original dyads. One member of each original dyad moves into an inner circle and is instructed to discuss any experiences relevant to both the two-member and four-member groups. His partner is now a member of the outer circle formed by all the partners. Members of the outer circle are instructed to observe their partner's interaction while they are in the inner circle. Five minutes. (6) The original dyads meet together; the observer offers feedback on the interaction of the participative partner. Five minutes. (7) The partner who acted previously as the observer then moves in with his counterparts to form a new inner circle and proceeds to discuss his experiences in the two-member and four-member groups. His partner is in the outer circle as an observer of his interactions. Fifteen minutes. (8) The original dyads come together again, and the member who was most recently in the inner circle receives feedback from his partner. Five minutes. (9) The group then meets as a whole for general discussion. Fifteen minutes.

This format is only an illustration. There are almost endless possibilities for human relations exercise designs; the program can adopt either previously published designs or create new ones to fit those group therapy learnings they wish to present through this format.

The T-group is another form of participative learning that can successfully be used in a group therapy training program. In fact, its presence can be instrumental in ensuring the program's success. Most of the procedures previously referred to require an atmosphere of trust, openness, and honesty between trainees, and between the trainees and their workshop leaders. Many programs report that attitudes of competitiveness and hostility among the students work against successful learning, and that classes, discussion groups, role playing, and student groups provide areas for destructive expression of resentment toward a training staff. The T-group defines the student as a participant, not as a patient, while the leader is defined as facilitator and not as an authority, expert, or doctor. The facilitator works with the group toward their achieving the identification and acceptance of positive and negative expressions, feelings, and reactions, and effective verbal and nonverbal communication. These achievements result in a sense of mutual trust among the members, openness of expression, and honesty in interpersonal relationships within the group.

"A supervised clinical experience is a *sine qua non* in the education of the group therapist" (Yalom, 1970, p. 376). The structure of supervision is varied. Most frequently the student acts as a therapist in his own group and has a supervisory session to match each of his group sessions. Or two students may serve as cotherapists, again with supervision given for each hour the group meets. In a third but less popular variation the student and supervisor act together as cotherapists with supervision occurring after the group session. The advantage of this third variation is that the supervisor is present during the group therapy experience. In the first two instances the supervisor must rely upon a less complete knowledge of what occurred in the group. This information is usually supplied in these cases by transcripts or tapes. Some programs try to overcome this disadvantage by providing a one-way mirror for observation.

Occasionally supervision is done in a group, with students sharing in the supervision. The advantage of group supervision is that it allows for a variety of interpretations of what is happening and of the therapeutic nature of the interventions. This variety may reduce the authoritarian nature of dyadic supervision, which because of this nature has been labeled a master and apprentice model. We believe that the therapy group does somewhat reduce the authoritarian nature of the dyadic relationship. Because group supervision is a model patterned after the experience the student is apprenticed to learn, the supervisors should break away from a one-to-one supervisory model that they themselves have learned in their original experiences with individual psychotherapy.

The problem of either designing or selecting a training program still remains to be discussed. We see the major issue involved here as one of training goals. What level of competence in group psychotherapy does the program wish to attain? This question is based upon who is recruited into the program and what his or her goals are. We discussed the question of the need and demand for practitioners earlier in this chapter, and pointed out that if only the highest educational standards of practice were maintained, the public need and clamor for therapeutic group experiences could not begin to be met by the carefully selected and exhaustively trained practitioner. The alternative to a small group of high-level therapists meeting only a fraction of public demand is most likely to be the burgeoning of self-styled, untrained practitioners. The rapid growth of the encounter movement administered by the untrained and partially trained is an immediate example of the kind of unfortunate and dangerous situation that can develop.

We propose that this issue can be moved toward satisfactory resolution through the utilization of the concept of levels of training. This is not a new concept and is already in practice; but it is desirable to recognize and encourage this trend. With this in mind we present two training programs here. The first is a program in group work training developed at Saint Elizabeth's Hospital (1966). This program was designed for staff members in the prevailing array of mental health disciplines. The educational requirements include a minimum of a bachelor's degree with courses leading to an understanding of sociological and psychological principles. The purpose of the program is "to further trainees in their career development as mental health professionals and to prepare them to function in the context of a mental health facility. To do this, the program is designed to assist trainees to develop competence in the use of group concepts and methods in the service of patients, and to integrate this group competence into their professional roles and in interaction with others."

The design of the program is as follows: In the initiation phase (phase 1), which lasts approximately eight weeks, students are given orientation, schedules, and assignments; they begin preparatory group supervision in on-going process groups, they observe a variety of groups; they discuss group observations in small task group meetings, and they attend intradisciplinary literature seminars arranged by discipline. In the differentiation phase (phase 2), of approximately nineteen weeks, the students continue group supervision in the on-going process groups; they begin individual supervision; and they attend classes on group psychotherapy, body movement and communication, and psychodrama. In the integration phase (phase 3), which lasts approximately eleven weeks, they continue group supervision in the on-going process group; they continue individual supervision; they continue group practice; they attend classes on interdisciplinary literature; and they take a final examination. After each phase students participate in a group evaluation.

Representative of the program for the more advanced student is one currently in use at the Post-Graduate Center for Mental Health in New York (Kadis, 1968). This program is designed for graduates of the psychoanalytic training program at the center and psychologists, psychiatrists, and psychiatric social workers from other analytic schools. The aim of the program is to offer sound training in group therapy techniques that would enable skilled individual psychotherapists already working in the usual dyadic relationship to enlarge their horizons and learn to alternate readily between the dyadic and the multiple triadic relationships, using the group as a therapeutic agent. The program is geared to run over a four-year period and requires the following theoretical and practical courses, seminars, and workshops: In the first year, Basic Concepts of Analytic Group Psychotherapy, Laboratory in Group Psychotherapy I, Continuous Group Case Seminar (both semesters), Group Psychodynamics in Group Psychotherapy, Personal Analytic Group Psychotherapy (the program provides for two years of Personal Analytic Group Psychotherapy for each candidate which runs for both semesters), Group Therapy Department Colloquium (both semesters), Treatment Planning in Combined and Conjoint Psychotherapy, Readings in Group Psychotherapy I, and Clinical Workshop in Multiple Transference Phenomena. In the second year, Research Seminar in Group Psychotherapy (both semesters), Utilization of Dreams, Fantasies, and Early Recollections in Group Analysis, Readings in Group Psychotherapy II, Group Therapy Department Colloquium (both semesters), Transference, Resistance, and Acting Out in Group Therapy, Personal Analytic Group Therapy (both semesters), Workshop in Counter Transference, Clinical Workshop in Working Through and Termination in Group Psychotherapy, Laboratory in Group Psychotherapy II. In the third year, Advanced Clinical Workshop (both semesters). In the fourth year, Theory and Techniques of Group Supervision (both semesters).

The two programs represent different levels of training. The first is designed for a mental health staff in a large psychiatric hospital, the second is designed for professionals who already have a high level of training in both the psychiatric and the psychoanalytic areas. These two examples serve as excellent models, but individual programs should be tailored to the training needs of the students and the goals of the programs.

Group psychotherapists have until recently not been concerned with special ethics for practitioners in their field, because practitioners have usually been members of regulatory associations and have used their association code of ethics as their guide to ethical behavior. The May 1973 Newsletter of the AGPA announced that the Committee on Ethics and Standards is presently at work on a reevaluation of the AGPA code of ethics since their membership may now include persons who are not members of regulatory associations or subject to a state licensing procedure. Also, there has been a concern expressed by AGPA members that the public may identify practitioners of other group methods, for example, T-group, psychodrama, and the encounter group, as group psychotherapists. AGPA has attempted to meet this problem in two ways: first, by formulating a basic code of ethics for its members, and secondly, by publishing a pamphlet titled *Consumer's Guide to Group Psychotherapy,* available in late 1973. This publication has as its major objective a definition of group psychotherapy, thus setting it apart from other forms of small group practice. The basic code of ethics appeared in the May 1973 Newsletter of the AGPA. It contains the following:

(1) The patient's health, integrity, and privacy are the therapist's primary professional interest. When these conflict with the personal, or commercial, or social interests of the therapist, agency, or institution, the patient shall be so informed.

(2) The group psychotherapist explains his procedures and goals to his patients and obtains their informed consent to these. He identifies clearly those procedures which are new or experimental, making their possible risks or advantages clear.

(3) The group psychotherapist obtains the best possible training available. He updates his training by reading, attending conferences, teaching, and being taught. He seeks consultation and supervision when indicated.

(4) The group psychotherapist, acting individually or as a member of an agency or institution, limits himself to the methods in which he has been trained, is being supervised, or is carefully researching.

(5) The group psychotherapist, if he proceeds with new or experimental methods, follows an established set of rules or guidelines as devised by the institution or professional body to which he belongs and should seek active consultation and supervision in so doing.

(6) The group psychotherapist shares his data and experiences in treatment, research, and training with the scientific community and the mental health professions.

(7) The AGPA and its members promote adherence to accepted ethical and scientific standards by means of education, publicity, peer group discussion, and corrective machinery.

Chapter VI

᚛᚛᚛᚛᚛᚛

Selecting and Training Trainers

As we have seen, the demand for small group experiences has been growing very rapidly and will probably continue for some time. This demand has resulted in attracting a variety of "helpers," with varying motivation, skills, knowledge, and experience. There are therapist-turned-trainer, clergymen-turned-trainer, architects-turned-trainer, housewives-turned-trainer, nurses-turned-trainer, graduate students-turned-trainer, student personnel staff-turned-trainer, managers-turned-trainer, teachers-turned-trainer, and so on, some with (and many without) adequate understanding of the requirements and responsibilities of the laboratory approach. Many individuals think that being a trainer provides a much simpler entry into a helping profession than being a therapist, for example.

The technologies readily available are deceptively simple: exercises, role-playing, intrapersonal dialogue, and so forth, which may be "learned" in one or more workshops. And there is always the unassailable justification by some self-selected "trainers" that "it feels right; therefore it is right." With the innocent complicity of the participants, in many groups feeling has replaced thinking; irrational behavior has come to be valued over rational behavior; and knowledge, evidence, and evaluation are often absent. In such cases, the trainer remains the unquestioned leader by virtue of his role; authority is never challenged; and both the scientific method and the democratic ethic are lost.

However, many people are searching for legitimate training experiences so they can become effective trainers and change agents. Let us assume that all of the people named in the first paragraph of this chapter do seek out further training and that new people entering the field do wish to find appropriate educational and training programs. Should there be any selection process? What criteria should be used for recruiting and/or selecting for training? In the 1946 Connecticut workshop the staff were all professionals to begin with. During the following two years they worked out a set of agreed upon objectives, clarified a common set of values, formulated a research program, and were trying to work from firm theoretical bases.

It will be recalled that originally it was hoped that effective change agents could be trained in the summer workshops by working toward an ambitious set of objectives, but very soon that became an impossible goal for a three-week experience. Only very recently has there been any real attention paid to the problems of how to prepare large enough numbers of trainers and consultants to meet the continuing demand and need, and how "professional" these people need to be. At this time there must necessarily follow a painful period of deselection of those already in the field, as well as inservice training and thoughtful and vigorous recruiting.

It may be useful to remember that the T-group and the laboratory represent *an alternative to the help-giving model,* and to see how this alternative is related to questions of recruiting, selection, and deselection. There are a variety of traditional help-giving relationships such as teacher-student, doctor-patient, parent-child, and minister-parishioner. Ordinarily these relationships have implied some *deficit or pain* on the part of the one being helped. And the deficit or pain is to be repaired by the helper whether the need is learning how to read or getting relief from neurotic symptoms.

The T-group helping relationship is based on a collaboration-among-peers problem-solving model in which all members participate. Everyone both gives and receives help. It rests implicitly on a theory of motivation and assumptions about the nature of human beings, which view people as proactive, competent, responsible, and growth-oriented, and it has required a theory of change appropriate to that orientation. As we have shown, we can let Maslow serve as the motivation theorist and Argyris as the change theorist at this time for selective, heuristic, and illuminative purposes, which may help us to define and elaborate educational and training programs as well as provide guides for selection.

Ideally, potential therapists *and* trainers would be drawn from a wide spectrum of educational experiences with an emphasis on behavioral science as a requisite part of that background. However, the kind of further training ought to be congruent with the orientation of the prospective leaders: primarily growth- and action-oriented, or primarily therapeutically oriented.

Broadly speaking, those who expect to be in roles which are relevant to therapy and will work with people who are seen as handicapped by deficits or pain—including some ministers and priests, some clinical psychologists, some social workers, some psychiatrists, some nurses, and so forth—will want an apprenticeship as therapists with therapists. This means that they will want to help individuals whose adaptive responses are ineffective, who are very unhappy with their own functioning, or worse still, are not functioning (that is, "patients" either in or out of institutional settings). As Parloff says: "The therapists' primary responsibility remains with patients—psychotic, schizoid, depressed, obsessive, compulsive, phobic, anxious, and sociopathic. He has no special responsibility or unique competence in dealing with others who have as their primary goals the seeking of a new purpose and meaning in life" (Parloff,

1970, p. 301). He adds that there are several classical prescriptions for the good life and people ought to have options to choose from.

Others then (including some ministers and priests, some clinical psychologists, some social workers, some psychiatrists, some nurses, and so forth) who are attracted to education, organizational development, community problems, and individual or institutional change through collaboration and help-sharing will want to be trainers. They will expect to work with educators, managers, community leaders, students, and any others who want to share responsibility in their work and community groups as well as learn about how these groups can become more effective, while they themselves become effective interpersonally and lead more satisfying lives. Unless we are to assume that everyone is operating from a deficit base and needs therapy, it can be agreed that an alternative model is at least desirable, if not essential.

Beyond that, however, we come back to the nature of the helping relationship: the one is help-giving and the other help-sharing. In the latter, we cannot repeat too often the importance of the democratic and scientific ethic and the differences in assumptions about human nature and motivation between traditional and laboratory learning. Both helping models are legitimate and both are needed. Some helpers may be able to use both orientations, but it would be very important first to understand the differences and to understand one's own motivation and preferred orientation. We are strongly urging that preprofessional choice take into account the differences between a help-giving and a help-sharing orientation as one's chosen mode and that professionals reassess their preferred orientation.

Laboratory training is an integral part of the field of applied behavioral science. It comes out of a tradition, represented by Kurt Lewin, that behavioral science and research ought to be integrally related to social action. This means an acknowledgement and an acceptance of the importance of a value system as an integal part of the theorist/researcher/practitioner. It means also a problem-solving approach and an orientation toward collaboration. These values or metagoals of laboratory training are perhaps the most important contribution the trainer brings to the group, and one ought to be as clear as possible about the implications of these requirements: an acceptance of the democratic ethic and the scientific ethic.

Now, before we look at a suggested model program of training, let us consider what the student trainee needs to know and be. First of all, we can look at the kinds of things a trainer (change facilitator) will need to know about groups. Basically, it is to be able to understand enough about what is happening to be able to make planned interventions and create learning opportunities for the participants to carry out their learning goals. It means, of course, first of all being able to create a learning environment which will allow participants to experience and utilize this alternative approach to interpersonal relations and intergroup relations. The student trainer needs to be able to articulate for himself a theory of human nature and know something about learning theory and change theory. He needs to understand something about individual dynamics and group dynamics. As was discussed in Chapter Four, this centers around communication, functional roles of group members, group problem-solving and decision-making, group norms and group growth, leadership and authority, and intergroup processes (particularly around the questions of competition and collaboration).

He needs to understand his personal dynamics and have some understanding of what his own strengths and weaknesses are in relation to the skills and knowledge required. This means also having some plan for continuing personal growth. It is important that he have a good deal of "free space" as compared with "hidden," "blind," and "unconscious" areas (see reference to the Johari Window in Chapter Four) so that his limitations do not impose too many restrictions on the group. It would be good to have some humility as well as an acceptance of, and willingness to use, his own competence and effectiveness. He also needs a philosophy as well as a training style; a commitment to a set of values which he has arrived at through a process of being aware of—and selecting from—a range of value options. This implies a commitment to the goals of the laboratory method: acceptance of a spirit of inquiry and a belief in collaboration. He needs to understand that there are different styles of training and that his techniques are related to his philosophy. Lomranz and Lakin (1970) have been concerned with this problem and have found confirmation of their hypothesis that there are three distinct trainer styles, each using different techniques toward different goals. These results are summarized in Table 10.

Trainers ought to know what their training philosophy, style, and goals are, and they should be as explicit about these as possible when describing what they do so that participants may choose those experiences which they will find meaningful and constructive. This means recognizing that training experiences are very closely tied to a value base and that it is a responsibility of the trainer to bring his stated intentions and his behavior as close together as possible.

It is timely to think about some minimum criteria for evaluating the competence of trainers, and how this competence can be acquired. Are there different "levels" of competence, that is, how can new and already practicing trainers assess their competence and pursue, and/or continue their professional development; how shall they select and find appropriate learning opportunities? More training programs should be developed as well as some cross-program agreement on standards of training. A list of some programs in existence is included later in this chapter; and the projected plans of the NTL Institute are outlined also. The Institute does intend to make professional training and development one of its important missions, and the plans obviously demonstrate that intention.

The need for professional trainers and for professional training obviously is very great. It will be important to encourage diverse sponsorship for these training programs simultaneously with an agreed-upon broad base of core requirements related to knowledge, skills, psychological readiness, supervised experience, ethical practices, and self-renewal plans which will insure effective and responsible practice. Selection and evaluation procedures also need to be developed.

It will be important for trainers of trainers to recognize that it is during that process that trainees will need to develop some important attitudes: (1) an attitude towards continued self-evaluation; (2) a recognition of responsibility to laboratory participants; (3) an understanding of the value system of the laboratory method, and a commitment to work for at least testing its viability; (4) an understanding and acceptance of theory and research as being in-

Table 10. Training Orientations of 138 Experienced Trainers

	Personal and Interpersonal Effectiveness and Learning (PIEL)	Personal and Interpersonal Remedial Experiences (PIRE)	Personal and Interpersonal Expanding Experiences (PIEE)
TRAINER GOALS	Focuses on interpersonal competence, organizational group dynamics, and social system effectiveness. Low priority for sensory awareness non-verbal communication, confrontation and intrapsychic processes.	Focuses mainly on personal needs and intrapsychic dynamics. Also on self-concept and trust development and on organizational group dynamics.	Expressiveness, intimacy, confrontation, trust development, sensory awareness. Low on intrapsychic dynamics.
TRAINER TECHNIQUES	Foster learnings about social system processes and relationships between them. Focus on interpersonal relationships or feed-back about group processes and consensual validation.	Oriented to the individual. Facilitate expression of emotions for remedial purposes. Also uses techniques of PIEL and PIEE.	Emotionally intense confrontations and nonverbal techniques. Also promote involvement, sometimes physical encounter, and stimulate fantasy.
PERSONAL VALUES; SELF-DESCRIPTION DATA	Favor social involvement, restraint and rationality. Lewinian and experienced as trainer.	Eclectic. Favor balanced life. Oldest in years and in training experience. Active and supportive.	Hedonistic values. Younger and less experienced. See self as energetic and dominant group leader. Rogerian, existential.

SOURCE: Adapted from an abstract of a study done by Jacob Lomranz and Martin Lakin, mimeo report, 3 pp., 1970.

tegrally related to practice, and at least a real willingness to collaborate with researchers (as opposed to an antiscientific attitude); (5) an appreciation for the importance of staff relations as a demonstration of the integration of metagoals with practice; (6) some understanding of the importance of collaboration among colleagues, as opposed to "doing one's own thing" in competitive isolation.

We suggest that the following factors be taken into consideration when selecting potential trainees: participation in at least two laboratories; written evaluation by professional staff members (for example, trainers in laboratories attended); self-assessment, including a statement of learning goals; education and familiarity with pertinent knowledge: either formal such as an advanced degree in behavioral science, or informal such as demonstrated familiarity—oral or written—with a minimum suggested reading list; and a personal interview to assess personal readiness with the trainee. Since this is a new and interdisciplinary profession that calls for personal as well as professional skills and experience, there is a need for alternative and nontraditional routes into the profession. Also, because the need is so great, it is necessary to make the best use of all potential resources and to be imaginative about how to provide the necessary training to supplement talents already possessed. In view of this, it is important to make training available for those individuals, sometimes called paraprofessionals, whose educational background would not normally qualify them for inclusion.

The training program itself should provide for education, training, and personal growth so that the trainer-in-training can later be qualified in the areas of knowledge, skills, personal readiness, experience, clinicing and supervision, and evaluation. The trainee will need *knowledge* in personality dynamics, psychopathology, group dynamics, social psychology, sociology, and change theory; that is, he needs to know what to look for in groups and how to make sense out of what he finds. In the area of *skills*, NTL (1968) points out three important components: analysis, planning and design, and application.

In *analysis*, the trainee needs the ability to understand and diagnose conditions which facilitate and inhibit learning and change in individuals and groups; ability to understand and diagnose his own needs and characteristics as these affect the nature and effectiveness of his relationship to client systems; ability to diagnose conditions affecting the operating effectiveness of groups (for example, power and communication relationships); and the ability to recognize difficulties which may develop in learning situations for individuals and groups and to use other resources as needed. In *planning and design,* the trainee needs the ability to plan and design human relations training laboratories for a range of learning goals and client systems; ability to design and develop a wide variety of experience-based training situations in response to learning needs of client systems; ability to design procedures for collecting and evaluating data on the functioning of client systems; ability to design and develop appropriate learning and change interventions within a variety of client systems. In *application,* the trainee needs to demonstrate ability to perform effectively as the responsible staff person in T-groups; demonstrated ability to work effectively in team situations; demonstrated effectiveness in working with a variety of groups; demonstrated ability to transmit ideas and concepts effectively; demonstrated ability to use a variety of exercises and technologies appropriately.

In terms of *personal readiness,* there are a number of desirable characteristics. Personal characteristics include openness to self and others; ability to grow (to stay a learner); being relatively unconflicted about authority and peer relations and in relation to sex, race, class, and other differences; ability to be a role model for participants; ability really to care for others and not to need to shape others to fit his own needs; and commitment to a set of values arrived at by choice (including a belief in the metagoals of the laboratory method).

The trainee ought to have a background of varied *experience,* including perhaps twenty laboratories as participant, observer, assistant trainer, and/or cotrainer with a variety of cotrainers and trainers; participation in a training-of-trainers program; good supervision and clinicing; other kinds of group experience for contrast such as teaching or coaching; and continued experience as a participant in personal growth and peer group labs. *Clinicing and supervision* should be regular and disciplined; that is, after each session we suggest a review of interventions of both trainers, a look at group development, a consideration of individual members'

change; and clinicing ought to include senior staff. After each
laboratory, senior staff ought to write an evaluation of each trainee's
participation including recommended further training. There should
be continued effort to keep communication open about the group
and the relationship between the cotrainers. Personal problems of
the trainee should be acknowledged, and recommendations for
therapy, personal growth laboratories, or other personal development experience or education, should be made.

After the trainee is in the program, there should be regular
evaluations, including self-evaluation (both personal and professional, that is, continuing self-renewal and growth plans); an assessment of training objectives and the development of a research
attitude; and access to continued education and supervision. In
addition, evaluation by participants, coleaders and supervisors, by
outside consultants and also through objective measures, before, during and after training, should be included. One way to look at the
training issue is to see the continuing development of a trainer over
time; this is summarized in Table 11. NTL plans for "learning
communities" (NTL, 1971, pp. 2–3) also are useful and are quoted
as follows:

> In the summer of 1971, the Institute will launch four
> *Learning Communities* which will represent a first step toward
> establishing year-round continuing education programs for
> professionals, specialists, and individuals. The objective is not
> only to provide quality training, but also to develop and test
> new training models and designs, and to research the training
> process.
>
> One section will begin with training individuals in the
> use of small group techniques, methods, skills, and knowledge.
>
> Another will be shaped to advance the knowledge and
> skill of those whose task it is to help organizations and indi-
> viduals use the power of change effectively. This group will
> work on problems of organizational development, power and
> control, conflict, consultation, negotiation, bargaining, the
> politics of change, examining the mix between the cognitive
> and emotional ingredients of decision-making and work pro-
> duction, and many others.
>
> A third thrust will begin a learning process that might
> be called "life style." The programs for this group will be

Table 11. DEVELOPMENTAL SCHEME FOR TRAINING AND PRACTICE

	A *Participant*	B *Beginning Trainer*	C *Intermediate Trainer*	D *Trainer of Trainers (advanced)*	E *Consultant (advanced)*
1. Experience	None required to enter.	Minimum of 2 previous labs for entry to program	20–25 labs acquired in training.	Varied experience as senior trainer and currently engaged in practice.	Same as col. D, row 1, plus supervised consultant experience.
2. Values and Metagoals	Willingness to experience alternative model of interpersonal relations.	Accept: a) spirit of inquiry b) collaboration c) authenticity d) freedom of choice for self and others.	Same as col. B, row 2	Same as col. B, row 2.	Same as col. B, row 2.
3. Attitudes, Behaviors	None required other than not too conflicted to participate fairly freely in here-and-now (not looking for therapy).	Demonstrate openness, risk-taking, role flexibility, ability to share in feedback, self-awareness.	Self awareness, psychological readiness as demonstrated in own interpersonal interactions (evident to peers), role flexibility, constructive interventions, shared leadership, good feedback.	Increase in col. C, row 3, evident to peers*.	Same as col. C, row 3; practices collaboration.

	A	B	C	D	E
4. Skills	Not relevant; will be introduced to and have practice in.	Develop learning plan for skill acquisition.	Application skills* Analytic skills*	Same as col. C, row 4, plus planning and designing skills; able to convey skills and supervise; skill evident to peers*.	Same as col. C, row 4, plus consultation skill.
5. Knowledge	Probably informal and limited; will be introduced to more formal conceptualization.	Formal and/or informal; begin to conceptualize systematically.	Formal and/or informal; advanced degree; knowledge organized; can demonstrate knowledge*	Formal and/or informal; advanced degree, knowledge organized around theory, can demonstrate knowledge*; contribute to knowledge.	Same as col. D, row 5.
6. Research	Openness to evaluation.	Ability to understand research, and willingness to provide data.	Cooperate with and/or contribute to research projects.	Contribute to evaluation of own and others' work.	Same as col. D, row 6.
7. Social Action	May already have interest in; or will be introduced to importance of.	Recognize need for.	Commitment to.	Commitment to and participation in.	Same as col. D, row 7.
8. Ethics	Develop awareness.	Introduced to ethical responsibility.	Accepts ethical responsibility; self-regulation.	Same as col. C, row 8.	Same as col. C, row 8.

* Eligible for accreditation.

designed to meet the needs of individuals. Included would be work on such matters as: life planning, coping with change and conflict, exploring new life-style models in families, marriages, communities, and so forth; effective volunteering, leisure living. Again, a major goal is for research and development, and experimentation for new models of learning.

The programs will begin in three geographical centers and will continue in several locations from time to time in the future. The faculty will be drawn from the most competent applied behavior scientists in the world. The intent is to create a community of learners who are committed to a continuing process which includes a diagnosis of needs and program development, related to each individual's life activity.

In 1973, a Center for Professional Development offering a broad range of programs year-round for professional development in the applied behavioral sciences was established. These are the groups of people for whom the programs are intended: organization members interested in tailor-made professional training in group leading skills or consultation skills for members of their organization; people without any previous laboratory experience; people with an introductory laboratory experience; graduate students enrolled in behavioral science or related programs; people who have completed some professional training in laboratory education or consulting skills and who have some professional experience in using this training; people who have participated in a previous learning community (or portion thereof); and established practitioners in the applied behavioral sciences (NTL, 1973).

The important point is that there is a need for continuing programs for personal and professional development in order to create effective change agents who can help individuals and institutions to improve the quality of living.

In 1962 the National Training Laboratories published a small volume on Issues in Training. At that time, the editors (Weschler and Schein) tried to bring together a series of articles which would stimulate further discussion and action about issues facing laboratory training. The "ferment and stimulation" they found then continue as the numbers of participants and trainers continue to increase exponentially. At the first workshop in Connecticut in 1946, there were six individuals from three institutions and the NEA involved in training. In 1962, there were over 100 individuals from over forty institutions. As of January 1971, there were about 600 fellows, associates and professional affiliates from several hundred institutions and other settings who were members of the NTL network. As Lubin and Eddy describe the training picture up to 1970:

> The first formalized internship program was held in Bethel during the summer of 1960. It combined participation in a laboratory, cotraining experience, and seminars on the various theoretical and methodological issues relevant to training. Subsequent intern programs have followed the same general format. Emphasis is placed upon competence in personal and interpersonal understanding and interaction, as well as mastery of cognitive material. Currently, NTL conducts internships in Applied Behavioral Science and in Group Leadership primarily for behavioral scientists interested in becoming professional trainers. In addition, there are a variety of programs in organization development, planned change, educational consultation, and community change intended for persons who plan to occupy training and consulting roles within their own organizational settings.
>
> A number of university graduate programs have also provided training techniques and related skills, either as a part of doctoral programs in social science fields or as an elective minor focus. Some of the schools that have, at varying times, provided trained personnel to the laboratory training field include Boston University, M.I.T., University of Michigan, UCLA, University of Cincinnati, Case Western Reserve University, and University of Kansas [Lubin and Eddy, 1970, pp. 322–323].

In the summer of 1973 about 200 people attended professional preparation programs sponsored by NTL.

Where shall all the trainers come from to meet the demand, however? Is training a profession and can we therefore look to professional schools to produce these trainers? Lippitt and This (1962) addressed the issue of the professional nature of training in 1960, and Schein and Bennis (1965) asked the same question several years later. To date it has not really been answered, but the field does seem to be moving inevitably in the direction of professionalization, with at least some of the motivation for professional status coming from a concern with financial and status rewards, as Lippitt and This were courageous enough to suggest, since these rewards are greater for the professions. But it is also an obvious way of protecting the public and insuring some minimum standards for practice. After reviewing several ways of trying to define profession, Lippitt and This arrived at the following criteria, arranged here in the order of frequency mentioned: "The profession has a body of specialized knowledge; the profession sets its own standards; its activities are essentially intellectual; the profession requires extensive preparation; the needed body of specialized knowledge is communicable; the profession places service above personal gain; the profession has a strong professional organization" (Lippitt and This, 1962, pp. 117–118). They went on to develop in some detail the essential areas of professional competence as they saw them and to offer some guideposts for trainer characteristics. The important conclusion they came to, which has been relatively ignored since then, is that training directors (about whom they were writing) should be learning theorists rather than merely training methodologists. At that time, they concluded that training had not yet reached professional status.

Later Schein and Bennis insisted that training must satisfy the requirements of a profession since training affects peoples' lives and attempts to change social systems. They also firmly state that any profession must meet certain criteria: "Professional practice must be founded on basic research and on reliable knowledge, that is, a profession must be scientifically based; a profession must enforce a codified system of ethics; a profession must be staffed by adequately trained and certified practitioners" (Schein and Bennis, 1965, p. 322). And they add that on all three counts questions must be raised about the professional status of laboratory training. More recently, the NTL issued a statement of standards (1970) for the use of laboratory method. It includes a statement of standards for trainers and consultants and guidelines to the public for evaluating competence, as follows: "(1) NTL Institute endorses the Ethical Standards of Psychologists of the American Psychological Association and urges its members to guide their conduct accordingly; (2) in relationships with individual clients and client groups, persons representing NTL Institute are expected to discuss candidly and fully goals, risks, limitations, and anticipated outcomes of any program under consideration; (3) NTL Institute trainers and consultants are expected to endorse the purposes and values and adhere to the standards presented in this paper" (NTL, 1970b, p. 10). They next added four other sets of standards covering skills, knowledge, experience, and personal growth.

There have been some regional and organizational attempts to move toward an understanding of standards for practice (for example, the New Hampshire Conclave on Ethics and Accreditation held in 1970), but the best-known "informal accreditation" has been recognition by NTL through membership in the Network. However, persons trained in other programs, such as the Boston University Human Relations Program, have been respected as trainers as well. Nevertheless the great expansion in the area of groups in the past few years, and the many less-than-fully qualified individuals and centers that have begun to move into the field, have made the move toward professionalization and accreditation a more urgent issue. Finally in 1971, NTL decided to give up its informal accreditation system (it stopped accepting anyone into the Network) and any plans to set up a formal branch of the organization to accredit. Instead, a new organization has been created, a professional organization called the International Association of Applied Social Scientists (IAASS). The organizing committee gave birth to itself and was chaired by the same Kenneth D. Benne who was involved in the first NTL workshop and who has for many years proposed such a separation of accreditation from training for NTL.

This new organization was incorporated in June 1971 and is composed of a Board of Trustees, a Committee on Standards and Admissions, a Committee on Ethics, and a Committee on Discipline. It also has regional peer review panels. Its two major functions are: "(1) To develop a certification process for organization and community development consultants, laboratory educators, and personal growth group consultants, which is based on a history of demonstrated competence in practice as seen by professional peers, supervisors, and clients; and (2) to educate the public regarding appropriate use of the applied social sciences, and responsible conduct of practitioners through the use of the mass media, community groups, educational systems, and the arts" (IAASS, 1972, p. 4).

Basically it is to be an association of peers who agree to share the responsibilities of recruiting, monitoring each other's work, and developing a code of ethics for this group of practitioners who will come from many disciplines and often belong to other professional organizations. There will be periodic reviews so that membership is not a permanent matter. It remains to be seen how inclusive it will become and how many practitioners will opt to join it. For one thing, the present accreditation fee of $200 may, in itself, discourage membership. In addition to accrediting Organization Development Consultants, Community Development Consultants, and Laboratory Educators, it has a division called Personal Growth Group Consultants which, as they say, "falls in the gray area of adult learning and therapy." Again it will be interesting to watch the development of this accreditation group to see if the encouter leaders choose to join.

Both the IAASS 1972 membership report and an NTL Task Force report (NTL, 1970) spell out types of accreditation procedures. The important variables are size of group, conceptual ability, and application effectiveness. Both organizations call for a reliance on peer evaluation; both utilize an initial screening by mail, based on self-evaluation of the candidate, and letters of recommendation from accredited professionals and others. The intention is to find out at this point if the candidate is altogether unqualified, if further training is required, or if the candidate can be accredited at the time of application. The second step proposed is a personal interview (although this step now is being by-passed by IAASS). The peer review panel makes the final decision, including any recommendations it has for further professional development of the candidate. At this time, IAASS is giving three-year and five-year accreditations. There are provisions for maintaining accreditation which assure that members, when accredited, stay in touch with new developments and maintain their quality of performance. This requires that standards of performance and of ethics be established as criteria by the accrediting organization.

Other accrediting arrangements probably will be made, perhaps regionally, while the profession is evolving. There are many people already in practice who may not meet the new requirements and also others who may not wish to join IAASS. Probably two to three years of planning and implementation are needed before accrediting machinery is relatively functional. But professionalization and accreditation are in the air and in the works, and are inevitable. Perhaps *this* organization, the IAASS, will know how to build in self-renewal plans (Gardner, 1965).

Ethical Issues

As was pointed out earlier, many quarters are concerned about what goes on in groups; and, at this time, the consequence is predictable: "legitimate" groups—with responsible trainers— must share the burden of being accountable for everything done in the name of the T-group, the sensitivity group, encounter groups, and so forth. Thus Maliver (1971), after a dramatic description of the suicide of a woman three months after beginning a continuing "encounter group" experience, describes in some detail "the encounter cult," and then near the end of the article refers to T-groups led by National Training Laboratories (which in a footnote he describes as "the earlier, more verbal form of encounter, or 'sensitivity training,' which has been commonly used in the corporate world") (Maliver, 1971). In this incidental association, all of the weight of the article falls on T-groups to bear the responsibility for a wide variety of therapy and encounter group objectives and implied "misdemeanors."

Other writers have also tried, sometimes objectively, sometimes not, to describe what goes on in groups. At times they seem to be critical from a "vested interest" point of view or out of ignorance. But many attempts are sincere efforts to appraise the uses and abuses of groups, and to help participants select wisely (Glueck, 1971; Gottschalk, 1971; Klaw, 1961; Siroka, Siroka, and Schloss, 1971).

Rogers has described some group leader practices that he does not think are constructive. His comments are reproduced here because they are relevant to the question of what is desirable and acceptable behavior for a trainer working in the framework of the laboratory method.

(1) I am definitely suspicious of the person who appears to be exploiting the present interest in groups. Because of the enormously expanding interest, a number of workers seem to me to have as their slogans, "Get publicity fast!" "Get on the bandwagon!" When such traits appear in individuals who are working with people, I am deeply offended.

(2) A facilitator is less effective when he pushes a group, manipulates it, makes rules for it, tries to direct it toward his own unspoken goals. Even a slight flavor of this kind can either diminish (or destroy) the group's trust in him, or —even worse—make the members his worshipful followers. If he has specific goals, he had best make them explicit.

(3) Then there is the facilitator who judges the success or failure of a group by its dramatics—who counts the number of people who have wept or those who have been "turned on." For me, this leads toward a highly spurious evaluation.

(4) I do not recommend a facilitator who believes in some single line of approach as the *only* essential element in the group process. For one, "attacking defenses" is the sine qua non. For another, "drawing out the basic rage in every person" is his one-note song. I have a great deal of respect for Synanon and the effectiveness of their work with drug addicts, but I am repelled by their hastily formed dogma that unrelenting attack, whether based on real or spurious feelings, is the criterion by which a group is to be judged successful or unsuccessful. I want hostility or rage to be expressed when it is present, and want to express them myself when they are genuinely present in me, but there are *many* other feelings, and they have equal significance in living and in the group.

(5) I cannot recommend as facilitator a person whose own problems are so great and pressing that he needs to center the group on himself and is not available to, nor deeply aware of, others. Such a person might well be a participant in a group, but it is unfortunate when he carries the label of facilitator.

(6) I do not welcome as facilitator a person who frequently gives interpretations of motives or causes of behavior in members of the group. If these are inaccurate they are of no help; if deeply accurate, they may arouse extreme defensiveness, or even worse, strip the person of his defenses, leav-

ing him vulnerable and possibly hurt as a person, particularly after the group sessions are over. Such statements as "You certainly have a lot of latent hostility," or "I think you're compensating for your essential lack of masculinity" can fester in an individual for months, causing great lack of confidence in his own ability to understand himself.

(7) I do not like it when a facilitator introduces exercises or activities with some such statement as, "Now we will all . . ." This is simply a special form of manipulation, but very difficult for the individual to resist. If exercises are introduced, I think any member should have the opportunity, clearly stated by the facilitator, to opt out of the activity.

(8) I do not like the facilitator who withholds himself from personal emotional participation in the group—holding himself aloof as the expert, able to analyze the group process and members' reactions, through superior knowledge. This is often seen in individuals who make their living by conducting groups, but seems to show both a defensiveness in themselves and a deep lack of respect for the participants. Such a person denies his own spontaneous feelings and provides a model for the group—that of the overly cool analytical person who never gets involved—which is the complete antithesis of what I believe in. That is what each participant will then naturally aim to achieve: the exact opposite of what I should hope for. Nondefensiveness and spontaneity—not the defense of aloofness—are what I personally hope will emerge in a group.

Let me make clear that I do not object at all to the qualities I have mentioned in any *participant* in the group. The individual who is manipulative, or over-interpretative, or totally attacking, or emotionally aloof, will be very adequately handled by the group members themselves. They will simply not permit such behaviors to continue persistently. But when the facilitator exhibits these behaviors, he tends to set a norm for the group before the members have learned that they can confront and deal with him as well as with each other [Rogers, 1970, pp. 66–68].

We may assume that most critics are searching for ways to identify competent trainers, training groups, and laboratories, and to help potential participants find appropriate experiences. They also are trying to bring to the attention of "professionals" the importance of recognizing the ethical implications of offering these kinds of experiences. As Lakin points out, there are ethical problems involved in setting up a group, in the conduct of a group, and following its termination. And he has made a very strong plea for professionalization; he also has outlined a set of training requirements that he believes would produce qualified professional trainers. He recalls the traditional values held by early trainers which included: "Concern for democratic processes and democratic change —which meant that 'individual and collective' awareness could forestall manipulation by dominant leaders or conformist tyranny by a group" (Lakin, 1969, p. 923).

Concerned about the evolution of "mutant forms of training," and the large number of poorly trained individuals setting themselves up as trainers, he makes a very strong plea for a number of safeguards. These include setting up professional association commissions; more immediately, the self-monitoring of legitimate trainers, after their attention has been brought to the importance of these problems. (Self-monitoring surely needs to be taught and modeled in the training of trainers, and built into the training program as a value.) He calls for a clear statement of standards of training, training preparation, and the publication of a code of ethics. It is critical for the trainer to understand his impact and to be prepared to help the members deal with it. He should not be meeting his own individual needs primarily. Lakin also describes some ethical issues which include seductive advertising and false promises; the need to deselect participants; the need to deselect trainers who have inadequate preparation; and unexamined trainer influence, intentional or unintentional.

Some examples of actual cases raising ethical issues are described by Cohen, Gadon, and Willits (1970).

(1) In a two-week human relations laboratory the staff was meeting for its planning sessions. When one staff member tried to raise some here-and-now issues with himself and other staff members and between other staff members, several of them responded with irritation. They told him that a staff meeting was not a T-group and that there was no need for processing relationships among the staff unless there were serious problems in getting the task done, which, they claimed,

was to outline the program for the two-week lab. When the time came for assigning cotrainers, one senior staff member said that he had just completed two, two-week labs in a row, and was very tired, so didn't want a cotrainer who would demand a great deal of clinicing time after the daily sessions. He maintained that 75 percent of what was said in the laboratory was bull-shit anyway and so he didn't want a cotrainer who would want to rehash the events of the day. As a consequence of these sentiments the staff planned the entire two-week lab, session by session, and finished in about half the days allotted for planning. They agreed to have the minimum possible number of meetings during the lab, though they did agree to have lunch together every day in order to exchange information about where the groups were.

(2) In a two-week basic human relations lab one of the staff members was a black clinical psychologist who had been recruited in an effort to increase participation by blacks in sensitivity training programs. Though he had conducted many group therapy sessions, his only previous experience with T-groups had been as a member, a year before, in a two-week lab. During the planning meetings he admitted that he knew very little about the exercises and design issues that the staff was discussing in preparation for the lab. When the question of possible assignment of cotrainers came up he nevertheless insisted that he did not want to have a cotrainer because he preferred to work alone.

(3) On the second day of the two-week human relations laboratory a female participant came to see one of the two trainers in the group. Though attractive, the girl was rather masculine and had arrived at the laboratory with a variety of sports equipment, such as tennis rackets, volley ball, baseball and bat, and so forth. She told the trainer that she wanted to have a talk because she was terribly hurt by the other trainer's casual mention during the day that he was married. The girl said that on the first night of the lab she had slept with the other trainer after having some drinks with him at the community room. She said that she was extremely upset by the fact that he had not told her explicitly that he was married when they had begun to talk. While she was complaining about this to the second trainer she was quite flirtatious in a way which could easily be interpreted as seductive. The

trainer wondered what exactly he should do and how he should respond to the girl.

(4) In an in-company training laboratory, one member revealed during one of the sessions that he was an overt homosexual. The trainer was also a consultant for the same company, and after the lab was asked by the man's superior and colleagues how he had done in the lab. During the questioning, the consultant realized that he suspected that the man was a homosexual and wanted confirmation.

(5) A young trainer had recently been to a three-hour demonstration of fantasy techniques. Soon after, he used the "walk around inside your body" exercise in a group where he was cotraining. He worked most closely with one member of the group while others were also instructed to fantasize in the same way. Late that night, a trainer from another group met a participant of the young trainer's group. She was walking around looking very distressed. When the trainer said, "Hi, how are you doing?" the girl responded by reporting that she was upset because she couldn't stop feeling that she was trapped inside her body; she hadn't been "released" from the exercise. Since the group session she had been unable to think of anything else.

Increasingly the *social system,* not the individual, is becoming the focus for change, and a *professional change facilitator* is emerging (Lubin and Eddy, 1970). Paralleling that shift will be an emphasis on organization development, formal and informal, with laboratory training methods focused on helping the organizations use their own resources for organizational renewal and problem-solving.

Another important development already touched on in earlier chapters is the increase in *temporary systems*—committees, teams, task forces, but also group marriages and other extended family arrangements as well as other group arrangements—more or less time-limited—for living, learning, working, and growing together. There is increasing recognition on the part of such groups that they need to recognize task and maintenance functions, and they are looking for facilitators and consultants who can help to make these experiments more viable (Appley and Clark, 1971).

Still another development concerns the new or renewed

commitment of behavioral scientists to work on social problems and the recognition that this means working through small groups as well. All these developments point to the increasing need for competent laboratory trainers and change facilitators whose value system is firmly based in the laboratory method and with an interest in changing the quality of life.

Bennis (1970) has some serious criticisms and qualifications to raise about planned change, however. In the first place he thinks change agents are fuzzy about what criteria of organizational effectiveness they are trying to optimize: legal, political, economic, technological, social, and/or personal. Beyond that he says:

> It is not all obvious to me that the types of change induced by the change agents are either (a) compatible with "human nature," or in accord with "findings from the behavioral sciences" as some change agents assert, or (b) desirable, even if they are in tune with man's need structure, or (c) functional.
>
> These new values which are espoused indicate a certain way of *behaving and feeling;* for example, they emphasize openness rather than secrecy, superior-subordinate collaboration rather than dependence or rebellion, cooperation rather than competition, consensus rather than individual rule, the rewards of team leadership rather than a one-to-one relationship with the boss, authentic relationships rather than those based on political maneuvering, and so on.
>
> Are they natural? desirable? functional? What then happens to status or power drives? What about those individuals who have a low need for participation and/or a high need for structure and dependence? And what about those personal needs which seem to be incompatible with these images of man, such as a high need for aggression and a low need for affiliation? In short, what about those needs which can be expressed and best realized through bureaucratic systems or benevolent autocracies? Are these individuals expected to be changed through some transformation of needs, or are they expected to yield and comply to a concept of human nature incompatible with their own needs? [Bennis, 1970, pp. 319–320]

Are these values "natural," "desirable," or "functional"?

There are many experiments in relating going on. As others have indicated, we are on the threshold of a possible revolution in human relations (Bugental, 1970; Otto, 1968; Reich, 1971; Roszak, 1969); and the model of collaboration: openness, caring, risk-taking, and so forth, appears to be the more appropriate model for interpersonal sharing of responsibility and intimacy through interdependence. *It ought to be available as one alternative.* Is this new way a viable option? *Can a human relations model coexist with the traditional power model?*

If the answer is not "yes" we may be very close to the third revolution: the one Kurt Vonnegut (1970) describes where managers, engineers, and machines take over to provide a world free of problems and free of human error (and choice). Obviously this alternative way of life, collaboration, needs all the help it can get, and the educating of change facilitators—laboratory trainers—is critical. They in turn will be able to help individuals develop their value systems, improve their skills, increase their knowledge, and turn their talents to the solution of urgent social problems.

As George Miller (1969) said in his presidential address to the American Psychological Society: "Anyone who reads the newspapers must realize that vast social changes are in the making, that they must occur if civilized society is to survive. Vested interests will oppose these changes, of course, but as someone once said, vested interests, however powerful, cannot withstand the gradual encroachment of new ideas. If we psychologists are ready for it we may be able to contribute a coherent and workable philosophy, based on the science of psychology, that will make this general agitation less negative, that will make it a positive search for something new."

In this connection, Robert M. Hutchins recently stated: "It seems probable that we are entering a post-industrial age in which the issue is not how to produce or even distribute goods, but how to live human lives; not how to strengthen and enrich the nation state, but how to make the world a decent habitation for mankind. The causes of the recent unrest among students are of course very complicated, but one of them is a feeling among young people that contemporary institutions . . . cannot in their present form deal with the dangers and opportunities of the coming age. The dangers are obvious enough, and the opportunities, though less often referred to, are equally great. The chance is there, the chance to have what Julian Huxley has called 'the fulfillment society,' and what others have called the learning society, or simply a human society. We have no very clear conception of what such a society would be like. But we have all learned from *1984* and *Brave New World* what some other possibilities are" (quoted in Douglas, 1970, pp. 15–16).

᷿᷿᷿᷿᷿᷿

Epilogue

The late 1960s and beginning of the 1970s have seen the development and proliferation of a significant number of alternative life styles. Many of these have included novel ways of living and working together; primary examples of this are seen in the commune, the "back to the land" movement, and experiments with group marriage. All of these can be seen as attempts at the creation of extended families and extended communities.

Philip Slater (1970, p. 5), one of the gurus of the counterculture, in his analysis of contemporary American society, recognizes that the desire for community, that is, "the wish to live in trust and fraternal cooperation with one's fellows in a total and visible collective entity," is deeply and uniquely frustrated by American culture.

Two other leading theoreticians of the counter-culture, Wilhelm Reich (1949) and Herbert Marcuse (1969), have strongly stated their belief that the reason vast numbers of people willingly accept their exploitation and give up their freedom lies in the character structure of society; that modern industrial states create needs and values that are then reproduced within every member of the society by the institution of the family. Reich calls for the end of the patriarchial family structure, Marcuse for new ways of personal relatedness. The counter-culture, in keeping with these views, has placed the modern American family under direct attack, both for its cult of individualism and for its furthering of the image of feminine domesticity.

A second human desire that seems deeply frustrated in the American culture is the desire for engagement, a need to come directly to grips with both social and interpersonal problems. Much has been written on the proliferation of serious public issues, the Vietnam War, the pollution problem, the concern with a virulent and pervasive racism, the threat of automation—and the individual's sense of powerlessness in the face of these problems.

Up until the late 1960s, evading and avoiding behaviors involving escape to the suburbs, to the automobile, and to other forms of privatism prevailed. Here again the change was heralded by youth and can be marked by the student demand for self-determination that was heard on the Berkeley campus of the University of California in 1964. Increasingly since then, however, the wish to become involved and engaged has been heard, not only from the campuses and the ghettos, but also from a growing number of ordinary citizens.

These needs for intimacy and engagement, which have been so frustrated by contemporary American culture, have made themselves felt in the ways people are perceiving and using both the T-group and the psychotherapy group. The T-group, perceived as an extension of the communal type of structure, is used to develop a sense of help-sharing and a feeling of intimacy between persons. The psychotherapy group is seen as a paradigm of the family structure and is used to work out unresolved nuclear conflicts whose repetitions in behavior have made for dissatisfaction in interpersonal relationships. The burgeoning of many intermediate group practices, such as the encounter group, growth group, and various experimental groups, represent attempts to redress both the difficulties attendant upon relatedness in the family and the seekings for the type of relatedness attributed to the commune. They may also be regarded as attempts to meet the growth needs of a developing mankind that needs no longer be survival-oriented.

Historically, mankind has vacillated between acceptance of two forms of social organization: the family, with its formal hierarchical structure, which seemed to be the organization of choice for the raising of children; and the communal peer-oriented organization, in which the aggrandizement of the individual at the expense of his fellows was a crime, which seemed to be the organization of adult society. The nuclear family has, in spite of recent attack, continued to maintain its position. But increasing mobility on the American scene has destroyed the communal aspects of life. In any single year, one of every four middle class families changes its geographical address. The stable local neighborhood is rapidly becoming a thing of the past, and the extended family is loosely bound together only by long-distance telephone.

The T-group can be viewed as an experimental paradigm for the functional community, its centrality lying in its attempt to provide a new way of being that meets the needs in a society where community has almost ceased to exist. It provides for group experience involving openness, risk-taking, the development of mutual trust, collaboration, and group problem-solving. The T-group can also be seen as a laboratory in which the business of learning how to find engagement takes place, an engagement which is modeled on the democratic ideal that each member's contribution has value and must be considered as a necessary part of any problem-solving enterprise.

Group psychotherapy, on the other hand, offers the participants a return to the family structure, a sort of second chance for adults to recombine in a family constellation where they can participate in a corrective emotional experience, which will, in effect, allow for a reliving of emotional traumas that have occurred within their own families of origin. These can be relived under the analytic eye of the therapist-parent who can utilize the transference phenomena to permit the patients to work through their emotional problems.

A present assessment of the field of group practice reveals significant departures from the original methods, aims, and limitations of both the T-group and the psychotherapy group. Encounter groups, sensitivity groups, growth groups, and experiential therapy groups have developed from these two original models. The more extreme fringes of these activities include theater games, sensory awareness groups, and Bach's fight therapy. Groups are organized with strangers, staff members, or patients. And finally, the traditional fifty-minute hour has been expanded to include the several-hour minithon and the twenty-four to forty-eight-hour marathon, while the three-week workshop has become contracted into the three-hour microlab. This development of new methods has not occurred in an orderly or controlled manner. Why then has this recent and sudden burgeoning of group practices come about? It is our contention that it has developed out of a recognition of a widespread popular demand for some interpersonal offering to combat the loneliness and alienation of the present era and help in the transition from a traditional competitive set of values to an emerging collaborative value system. That practitioners from the group psychotherapy and T-group fields have greatly modified their original practices to meet this "cry from the heart" is an all-too-human response of those engaged in the helping professions to offer relief; but these modifications are not necessarily the help that is needed.

It is necessary to enter a caveat here. The therapy group offers the participant an opportunity to remediate emotional difficulties arising from family experiences, while the T-group offers an opportunity for the participant to experience collaborative problem-solving. Both group experiences are preparatory for more successful life experiences in society. Neither, however, is designed to take the place of real-life groups. There are limits to the efficacy of group practice, and the learnings must be transferable. For example: T-group participants may go out and act as change agents to bring about a society that is more communally oriented. Participation in the psychotherapy group may free some women to go out and demand recognition of their potential from a begrudging culture. We therefore, underscore our concern that group practitioners ought not overadvertise their goals nor overextend their methodology to promise more than they can realistically or ethically deliver, and they should help participants to recognize their own responsibilities for using their learnings outside the group, if these changes in attitudes and behaviors are to be effective.

ҡҡҡҡҡҡ

Bibliography

ACKERMAN, N. *The Psychodynamics of Family Life.* New York: Basic
    Books, 1958.
ALBEE, G. W. "The Uncertain Future of Clinical Psychology." *Ameri-
    can Psychologist,* 1970, *4,* 1071–1080.
ALEXANDER, F. G., and FRENCH, T. M. *Psychoanalytic Therapy: Prin-
    ciples and Application.* New York: Ronald Press, 1946.
AMERICAN GROUP PSYCHOTHERAPY ASSOCIATION, STANDARDS AND
    ETHICS COMMITTEE. *The Competence and Training of Group
    Psychotherapists.* New York, 1966.
AMERICAN GROUP PSYCHOTHERAPY ASSOCIATION, STANDARDS AND
    ETHICS COMMITTEE. *Group Psychotherapy Training Centers: A*

189

Guide to Professional and Educational Qualifications of Candidates and Content of Training Programs. New York, 1968.

APPLEY, D. G., and CLARK, T. "The Rise and Fall of Almost Every Alternative," Amherst, Mass., 1971.

APPLEZWEIG, D. G. "Some Determinants of Behavioral Rigidity." *Journal of Abnormal and Social Psychology,* 1954, *49,* 224–228.

ARGYRIS, C. *Integrating the Organization and the Individual.* New York: Wiley, 1964.

ARGYRIS, C. "Explorations in Interpersonal Competence—I and II." *Journal of Applied Behavioral Science,* 1965, *1,* 58–83, 255–269.

ARGYRIS, C. "Conditions for Competence Acquisition and Therapy." *Journal of Applied Behavioral Science,* 1968, *4,* 147–177.

ARGYRIS, C. "The Incompleteness of Social-Psychological Theory." *American Psychologist,* 1969, *24,* 893–908.

AZIMA, F. J. "Interaction and Insight in Group Psychotherapy: The Case for Insight." *International Journal of Group Psychotherapy,* 1969, *19,* 259–267.

BALES, R. F. *Interaction Process Analysis.* Cambridge: Addison-Wesley, 1950.

BATESON, G., and RUESCH, J. *Communication, the Social Matrix of Psychiatry.* New York: Norton, 1951.

BEDNAR, R. L. "Group Psychotherapy Research Variables." *International Journal of Group Psychotherapy,* 1970, *20,* 146–152.

BENNE, K. D. "History of the T-Group in the Laboratory Setting." In L. P. Bradford, J. R. Gibb, and K. D. Benne (Eds.), *T-Group Theory and Laboratory Method: Innovation in Re-education.* New York: Wiley, 1964a.

BENNE, K. D. "From Polarization to Paradox." In L. P. Bradford, J. R. Gibb, and K. D. Benne (Eds.), *T-Group Theory and Laboratory Method: Innovation in Re-education.* New York: Wiley, 1964b.

BENNE, K. D., and SHEATS, P. "Functional Roles of Group Members." *Journal of Social Issues,* 1948, *4,* 41–49.

BENNIS, W. G. "Patterns and Vicissitudes in T-Group Development." In L. P. Bradford, J. R. Gibb, and K. D. Benne (Eds.), *T-Group Theory and Laboratory Method: Innovation in Re-education.* New York: Wiley, 1964.

BENNIS, W. G. *Changing Organizations.* New York: McGraw-Hill, 1966.

BENNIS, W. G. "Beyond Bureaucracy." In W. G. Bennis and P. S. Slater (Eds.), *The Temporary Society*. New York: Harper and Row, 1968a.

BENNIS, W. G. "The Temporary Society." In W. G. Bennis and P. S. Slater (Eds.), *The Temporary Society*. New York: Harper and Row, 1968b.

BENNIS, W. G. "Goals and Meta-goals." In C. R. Mill (Ed.), *Selections from Human Relations Training News*. Washington, D.C.: NTL, 1969.

BENNIS, W. G. "The Change Agents." In R. T. Golembiewski and A. Blumberg (Eds.), *Sensitivity Training and the Laboratory Approach: Readings About Concepts and Applications*. Itasca, Ill.: Peacock, 1970.

BENNIS, W. G., and SHEPARD, H. A. "A Theory of Group Development." *Human Relations*, 1956, *9*, 415–437.

BENNIS, W. G., and SLATER, P. S. *The Temporary Society*. New York: Harper and Row, 1968.

BERNE, E. *Games People Play: The Psychology of Human Relationships*. New York: Grove Press, 1964.

BERZON, B., REISEL, J., and DAVIS, D. P. *PEER: Planned Experiences for Effective Relating*. An audio-tape program for self-directed small groups. La Jolla, Calif.: Western Behavioral Sciences Institute, 1969.

BION, W. R. *Experiences in Groups*. London: Tavistock, 1961.

BIRNBAUM, M. "Sense and Nonsense About Sensitivity Training." *Saturday Review*, Nov. 15, 1969, pp. 82–83, 96–98.

BLAKE, R. R. "Studying Group Action." In L. P. Bradford, J. R. Gibb, and K. D. Benne (Eds.), *T-Group Theory and Laboratory Method: Innovation in Re-education*. New York: Wiley, 1964.

BLAKE, R. R., and MOUTON, J. S. "The Instrumented Training Laboratory." In I. R. Weschler and E. H. Schein (Eds.), *Issues in Human Relations Training. Selected Reading Series #5*. Washington, D.C.: NTL, 1962.

BLAKE, R. R., and MOUTON, J. S. *The Managerial Grid*. Houston: Gulf, 1964.

BLAKE, R. R., SHEPARD, H. A., and MOUTON, J. S. *Intergroup Conflict in Organizations*. Ann Arbor, Mich.: Foundation for Research in Human Behavior, 1964.

BRADFORD, L. P. "Membership and the Learning Process." In L. P. Bradford, J. R. Gibb, and K. D. Benne (Eds.), *T-Group*

Theory and Laboratory Method: Innovation in Re-education. New York: Wiley, 1964.

BRADFORD, L. P. "Biography of an Institution." *Journal of Applied Behavorial Science,* 1967, *3,* 127–143.

BRADFORD, L. P., GIBB, J. R., and BENNE, K. D. (Eds.) *T-Group Theory and Laboratory Method: Innovation in Re-education.* New York: Wiley, 1964a.

BRADFORD, L. P., GIBB, J. R., and BENNE, K. D. "Two Educational Innovations." In L. P. Bradford, J. R. Gibb, and K. D. Benne (Eds.), *T-Group Theory and Laboratory Method: Innovation in Re-education.* New York: Wiley, 1964b.

BRADFORD, L. P., GIBB, J. R., and BENNE, K. D. "A Look to the Future." In L. P. Bradford, J. R. Gibb, and K. D. Benne (Eds.), *T-Group Theory and Laboratory Method: Innovation in Re-education.* New York: Wiley, 1964c.

BUCHANAN, P. "Evaluating the Effectiveness of Laboratory Training in Industry." *An Exploration in Human Relations Training and Research,* Report #1. Washington, D.C.: NTL, 1965.

BUCHANAN, P. "Laboratory Training and Organization Development." *Administrative Science Quarterly,* 1969, *40,* 466–480.

BUGENTAL, J. F. T. *Challenges to Humanistic Education.* New York: McGraw-Hill, 1967.

BUGENTAL, J. F. T. and TANNENBAUM, R. "Sensitivity Training and Being Motivation." *Journal of Humanistic Psychology,* 1963, 76–85.

BURROW, T. "The Group Method of Analysis." *Psychoanalytic Review,* 1927, *14,* 268–280.

BURTON, A. *Encounter.* San Francisco: Jossey-Bass, 1969.

CAMPBELL, J. P., and DUNNETTE, M. D. "Effectiveness of T-Group Experiences in Managerial Training and Development." *Psychological Bulletin,* 1968, *70,* 73–104.

CARTWRIGHT, D., and ZANDER, A. (Eds.) *Group Dynamics: Research and Theory.* Evanston, Ill.: Row, Peterson, 1953, pp. 287–301.

CLARK, J., and CULBERT, S. A. "Mutually Therapeutic Perception and Self-Awareness in a T-Group." *Journal of Applied Behavioral Science,* 1965, *1,* 180–194.

CLARK, J. V. "Authentic Interaction and Personal Growth in Sensitivity Training Groups." *Journal of Humanistic Psychology,* 1963, *2,* 1–13.

COHEN, A. R., GADON, H., and WILLITS, R. D. "Some Actual Cases Raising Ethical Issues." 1970.

CORSINI, R. J. "Immediate Therapy in Groups." In G. M. Gazda (Ed.), *Innovations to Group Psychotherapy*. Springfield, Ill.: Charles C. Thomas, 1970.

CRANSHAW, R. "How Sensitive is Sensitivity Training?" *American Journal of Psychiatry*, 1969, *126*, 136–141.

DALLAS GROUP PSYCHOTHERAPY SOCIETY. *Group Psychotherapy Training Program*. Dallas, 1965.

DAVIS, F. B., and LOHR, N. H. "Special Problems with the Use of Co-therapists in Group Psychotherapy." *International Journal of Group Psychotherapy*, 1971, *21*, 143–158.

DAVIS, S. A. "An Organic Problem Solving Method of Organizational Change." *Journal of Applied Behavioral Science*, 1967, *5*, 3–21.

DIMOCK, H. G. *How to Observe Your Group*. Montreal: Sir George William University, 1970.

DOUGLAS, W. O. *Points of Rebellion*. New York: Vintage, 1970.

DURHAM, L. E., GIBB, J. R., and KNOWLES, E. C. "A Bibliography of Research (1947–60; 1960–67)." In *Explorations in Applied Behavioral Science*, New York: NTL, Renaissanse Editions, Inc., 1967.

DYER, W. G. "An Inventory of Trainer Interventions." In C. R. Mill (Ed.), *Selections from Human Relations Training News*. Washington, D.C.: NTL, 1969.

EGAN, G. *Encounter: Group Processes for Interpersonal Growth*. Belmont, Calif.: Brooks/Cole, 1970.

ERIKSON, E. H. *Childhood and Society*. New York: Norton, 1959.

ERIKSON, E. H. "Youth: Fidelity and Diversity." *Daedalus*, 1962, *91, 1*, 5–27.

EZRIEL, H. "A Psychoanalytic Approach to Group Treatment." *British Journal of Medical Psychology*, 1950, *23*, 59–74.

EZRIEL, H. "The Role of Transference in Psychoanalytical and Other Approaches to Group Treatment." *Acta Psychotherapy*, 1957, *7*, 101–116.

FENICHEL, O. *The Psychoanalytic Theory of Neurosis*. New York: Norton, 1945.

FINK, S. L. "Thoughts on Interpersonal Communication and Group Climate." *Human Relations Training News*, 1968, *12*, 1–4.

FOULKES, S. H. *Therapeutic Group Analysis*. New York: International Universities Press, 1964.

FREUD, S. *Group Psychology and the Analysis of the Ego*. In Complete Works, Vol. 18. London: Hogarth Press, 1922.

FROMM, E. *Escape from Freedom*. New York: Rinehart, 1941.

GARDNER, J. W. *Self Renewal: The Individual and the Innovative Society.* New York: Harper Colophon Edition, 1965.

GARDNER, J. W. *No Easy Victories.* New York: Harper Colophon Books, Inc., 1969.

GERTZ, B. "Trainer Role versus Therapist Role." In C. R. Mill (Ed.), *Selections from Human Relations Training News.* Washington, D.C.: NTL Institute, 1969.

GIBB, J. R. "The Present Status of T-Group Theory." In L. P. Bradford, J. R. Gibb, and K. D. Benne (Eds.), *T-Group Theory and Laboratory Method: Innovation in Re-education.* New York, Wiley, 1964a.

GIBB, J. R. "Climate for Trust Formation." In L. P. Bradford, J. R. Gibb, and K. D. Benne (Eds.), *T-Group Theory and Laboratory Method: Innovation in Re-education.* New York: Wiley, 1964b.

GIBB, J. R. "The Effects of Human Relations Training." In A. E. Bergin and S. L. Garfield (Eds.), *Handbook of Psychotherapy and Behavior Change.* New York: Wiley, 1972.

GLUECK, W. F. "Reflections on a T-Group Experience." In R. W. Siroka, E. K. Siroka, and G. A. Schloss (Eds.), *Sensitivity Training and Group Encounter.* New York: Grosset and Dunlap, 1971.

GOLEMBIEWSKI, R. T., and BLUMBERG, A. (Eds.) *Sensitivity Training and the Laboratory Approach: Readings about Concepts and Applications.* Itasca, Ill.: Peacock, 1970.

GOTTSCHALK, L. A. "Psychoanalytic Notes on T-Groups in the Human Relations Laboratory, Bethel, Maine." In R. W. Siroka, E. K. Siroka, and G. A. Schloss (Eds.), *Sensitivity Training and Group Encounter.* New York: Grosset and Dunlap, 1971.

GOTTSCHALK, L. A., AND PATTISON, E. M. "Psychiatric Perspectives on T-Groups and the Laboratory Movement—an Overview." *American Journal of Psychiatry,* 1969, *126,* 91–107.

HAMPDEN-TURNER, C. M. "An Existential 'Learning Theory' and the Integration of T-Group Research." *Journal of Applied Behavioral Science,* 1966, *2,* 367–386.

HARRIS, T. G. "Warren Bennis—a Conversation." *Psychology Today,* 1970, *3.*

HARRISON, R. "Group Composition Models for Laboratory Design." *Journal of Applied Behavioral Science,* 1965, *1,* 409–32.

HARRISON, R. *Explorations in Applied Behavioral Science: Part 1. Problems in the Design and Interpretation of Research on*

Human Relations Training. New York: NTL, Renaissance
Editions, Inc., 1968.

HARRISON, R. "Training Designs for Intergroup Collaboration." In
C. R. Mill (Ed.), *Selections from Human Relations Training
News.* Washington, D.C.: NTL, 1969.

HORWITZ, M. "Training in Conflict Resolution." In L. P. Bradford,
J. R. Gibb, and K. D. Benne (Eds.), *T-Group Theory and
Laboratory Method: Innovation in Re-education.* New York:
Wiley, 1964a.

HORWITZ, M. "Transference in Training Groups and Therapy Groups."
International Journal of Group Psychotherapy, 1964b, *14,* 202–
213.

HOUSE, R. J. "T-Group Education and Leadership Effectiveness: A
Review of the Empirical Literature." *Personnel Psychology,*
1967a, *20,* 1–32.

HOUSE, R. J. "Manager Development: A Conceptual Model, Some
Propositions and a Research Strategy for Testing the Model."
In *Management Development: Design, Evaluation and Imple-
mentation.* Ann Arbor: University of Michigan, 1967b.

HOWARD, J. *Please Touch!* New York: Dell, 1971.

HUXLEY, J. (Ed.) *The Humanist Frame.* London: George Allen and
Unwin, 1961.

IAASS. "Policies and Procedures for Accredited Membership," 1972.
1755 Massachusetts Ave. N.W., Suite 300, Washington, D.C.,
20036.

JENKINS, D. H. "How Training Groups Work." Philadelphia, Pa.:
Temple University, 1967.

KADIS, A. L. *Current Models in the Training of Group Psychotherapists: The Training of Group Psychotherapists at the Post-
Graduate Center for Mental Health, New York City.* Paper
presented at American Group Psychotherapy Meeting, Chicago,
January 1968.

KAPP, F., GLASER, C., BRISSENDEN, A., EMERSON, R., WINGT, J. and
KASHDAN, B. "Group Participation and Self-Perceived Personality Change." *Journal of Nervous and Mental Disease,* 1964,
193, 255–265.

KLAW, S. "Two Weeks in a T-Group." *Fortune,* 1961, *64,* 114–117.

KOCH, S. "The Image of Man Implicit in Encounter Group Theory."
Journal of Humanistic Psychology, 1971, *11* (2), 109–127.

KOLB, D. A., and BOYATZIS, R. E. "On the Dynamics of the Helping

Relationship." *Journal of Applied Behavioral Science,* 1970, *6,* 267–290.

KUEHN, J. L., and CRINELLA, F. M. "Sensitivity Training: Interpersonal 'Overkill' and Other Problems." *American Journal of Psychiatry,* 1969, *126,* 108–118.

KURILOFF, A. H., and ATKINS, S. "T-Group for a Work Team." *Journal of Applied Behavioral Science,* 1966, *2,* 63–94.

LAING, R. D. *The Politics of the Family.* Toronto: Hunter Rose, 1971.

LAKIN, M. "Some Ethical Issues in Sensitivity Training." *American Psychologist,* 1969, *24,* 921–928.

LAKIN, M., LIEBERMAN, M. A., and WHITAKER, D. D. "Issues in the Training of Group Psychotherapists." *International Journal of Group Psychotherapy,* 1969, *19,* 307–325.

LAZELL, E. W. "The Group Treatment of Dementia Praecox." *Psychoanalytic Review,* 1921, *8,* 168–179.

LEWIN, K. "Group Decision and Social Change." In T. Newcomb and E. Hartley (Eds.), *Readings in Social Psychology.* New York: Holt, Rinehart and Winston, 1947.

LEWIN, K. "Studies in Group Decision" in D. Cartwright and A. Zander (Eds.), *Group Dynamics: Research and Theory.* Evanston, Ill.: Row, Peterson, 1953, pp. 287–301.

LIEBERMAN, M., and GARDNER, J. W. *Function of the Human Potential Movement.* Chicago: University of Chicago, 1973.

LIKERT, R. *The Human Organization.* New York: McGraw-Hill, 1967.

LIPPITT, R., and WHITE, R. K. "An Experimental Study of Leadership and Group Life." In E. E. Maccoby, T. M. Newcomb and E. E. Hartley (Eds.), *Readings in Social Psychology.* New York: Henry Holt, 1958.

LIPPITT, R. L., and THIS, L. E. "Is Training a Profession?" In I. R. Weschler and E. H. Schein (Eds.), *Issues in Human Relations Training,* Vol. 5. Washington, D.C.: NTL, 1962.

LOMRANZ, J., and LAKIN, M., "Variants in Group Sensitivity Training and Encounter." Abstract and letter. Durham, N.C.: Duke University, 1970.

LUBIN, B., and EDDY, W. B. "The Laboratory Training Model: Rationale, Method and Some Thoughts for the Future." *International Journal of Group Psychotherapy,* 1970, *20,* 305–339.

LUFT, J. *Group Processes: An Introduction to Group Dynamics.* Palo Alto, Calif.: The National Press, 1963.

LUFT, J. "Structural Interventions." In C. R. Mill (Ed.), *Selections from Human Relations Training News,* Washington, D.C.: NTL, 1969.

MAC LENNON, B. W., and LEVY, N. "Group Psychotherapy Literature 1967." *International Journal of Group Psychotherapy,* 1968, *18,* 375–401.

MAC LENNON, B. W., and LEVY, N. "The Group Psychotherapy Literature 1968." *International Journal of Group Psychotherapy,* 1969, *19,* 382–408.

MALIVER, B. L. "Encounter Groupers Up Against the Wall." *New York Times Magazine,* Jan. 3, 1971, pp. 4–5, 37–41, 43.

MARCUSE, H. *Essay on Liberation.* Boston: Beacon Press, 1969.

MANN, R. D. *Interpersonal Styles and Group Development: An Analysis of the Member-Leader Relationship.* New York: Wiley, 1967.

MARROW, A. J. *Behind the Executive Mask.* New York: American Management Association, 1964.

MARROW, A. J. "Events Leading to the Establishment of the National Training Laboratories." *Journal of Applied Behavioral Sciences,* 1967, *3,* 144–150.

MARROW, A. J. *The Practical Theorist.* New York: Basic Books, 1969.

MARSH, L. C. "Group Treatment by the Psychological Equivalent of the Revival." *Mental Hygiene,* 1931, *15,* 328–349.

MARSH, L. C. "Group Therapy in the Psychiatric Clinic." *Journal of Nervous and Mental Diseases,* 1935, *82,* 381–392.

MASLOW, A. H. *Toward a Psychology of Being.* New York: Van Nostrand, 1962.

MASLOW, A. H. *Motivation and Personality* (2nd ed.) New York: Harper and Row, 1970.

MAY, R. *Love and Will.* New York: Norton, 1969.

MC GREGOR, D. *The Human Side of Enterprise.* New York: McGraw-Hill, 1960.

MILES, M. B. *Learning to Work in Groups.* New York: Teachers College, Columbia University, 1959.

MILES, M. B. "Changes During and Following Laboratory Training: A Clinical Experimental Study." *Journal of Applied Behavioral Sciences,* 1965, *1,* 215–242.

MILLER, E. G., and RICE, A. K. *Systems of Organizations.* London: Tavistock, 1967.

MILLER, G. A. "Psychology as a Means of Promoting Human Welfare," Presidential address to the American Psychological Association. Sept. 1969.

MILLS, T. M. *Group Transformation: An Analysis of a Learning Group.* Englewood Cliffs, New Jersey: Prentice Hall, 1964.

MULLAN, H., and ROSENBAUM, M. *Group Psychotherapy.* New York: Free Press, 1962.

NADLER, E. B. "A Theory of Disconfirmation." In C. R. Mill (Ed.), *Selections from Human Relations Training News.* Washington, D.C.: NTL, 1969.

NATIONAL TRAINING LABORATORIES. "Suggested Qualifications for Trainers." Washington, D.C.: NTL, 1968.

NATIONAL TRAINING LABORATORIES. *Readings for Annual Laboratories in Human Relations Training,* Washington, D.C.: NTL, 1969.

NATIONAL TRAINING LABORATORIES. *Readings for Annual Laboratories in Community Leadership Training,* Washington, D.C.: NTL, 1970a.

NATIONAL TRAINING LABORATORIES. *Standards for the Use of the Laboratory Method.* Washington, D.C.: NTL, 1970b.

NATIONAL TRAINING LABORATORIES. "Professional Development Learning Communities." Washington, D.C.: NTL, 1970c.

NATIONAL TRAINING LABORATORIES. "Task Force Proposal Regarding Accreditation." In *Report of Task Force on Network Reorganization.* Washington, D.C.: NTL, 1970d.

NATIONAL TRAINING LABORATORIES. "The NTL Institute Future." Washington, D.C.: NTL, 1971.

NATIONAL TRAINING LABORATORIES. "Center for Professional Development Program Descriptions," Washington, D.C.: NTL, 1973.

ODIORNE, G. J. "The Trouble with Sensitivity Training." *Training Directors' Journal (Journal of the American Society of Training Directors),* 1963, *17,* 9–20.

O'HEARNE, J. J., AND GLAD, D. G. "Interaction and Insight in Group Psychotherapy: The Case for Interaction." *International Journal of Group Psychotherapy,* 1969, *19,* 268–278.

OTTO, H. A. *Human Potentialities: The Challenge and the Promise.* St. Louis: Warren H. Green, 1968.

PARLOFF, M. B. "Group Therapy and the Small Group Field: An Encounter." *International Journal of Group Psychotherapy,* 1970, *20,* 265–304.

PECK, H. B., and SCHEIDLINGER, S. "The Group in Education, Group Work and Psychotherapy—Round Table, 1953." *American Journal of Orthopsychiatry,* 1954, *24,* 128–52.

PERLS, F. S. *Gestalt Therapy Verbatim.* Lafayette, Calif.: Real People Press, 1969.

PFEIFFER, J. W., AND JONES, J. E. *A Handbook of Structured Experiences for Human Relations Training*. Vol. I, Iowa City: University Associates Press, 1969.

POWDERMAKER, F., AND FRANK, J. D. *Group Psychotherapy*. Cambridge: Harvard University Press, 1953.

PRATT, J. H. "The Class Method of Treating Consumption in the Homes of the Poor." *Journal American Medical Association*, 1907, *49*, 755–759.

PRATT, J. H. "The Use of Dejerine's Methods in the Treatment of the Common Neurosis by Group Psychotherapy." *Bulletin New England Medical Center*, 1913, *15*, 1–9.

PSATHAS, G., AND HARDERT, R. "Trainer Interventions and Normative Patterns in the T-Group." *Journal of Applied Behavioral Science*, 1966, *2*, 149–169.

RAKSTIS, T. J. "Sensitivity Training: Fad, Fraud, or New Frontier?" *Today's Health*, Jan. 1970, pp. 20–25, 86–87.

REDL, F. *When We Deal With Children*. New York: Free Press, 1966.

REICH, C. G. *The Greening of America*. New York: Bantam, 1971.

REICH, W. *Character Analysis*. New York: Farrar, Straus and Giroux, 1949.

REISEL, J. "Observations on the Trainer Role: A Case Study." In I. R. Weschler and E. H. Schein (Eds.), *Issues in Training Series #5*. Washington, D.C.: NTL, 1962.

RICE, A. K. *The Enterprise and Its Environment*. London: Tavistock, 1963.

RICE, A. K. *Learning for Leadership*. London: Tavistock, 1965.

RIOCH, M. J. "Group Relations: Rationale and Techniques." *International Journal of Group Psychotherapy*, 1969, *23*, 340–355.

ROGERS, C. R. *Encounter Groups*. New York: Harper and Row, 1970.

ROSZAK, T. *The Making of a Counter Culture*. New York: Doubleday, 1969.

SAINT ELIZABETH'S HOSPITAL. *Group Work Training*. Washington, D.C., 1966.

SANFORD, N. "Whatever Happened to Action Research?" *Journal of Social Issues*, 1970, *26*, 3–23.

SATIR, V. *Conjoint Family Therapy: A Guide to Theory and Technique*. Palo Alto: Science and Behavior Books, Inc., 1964.

SCHEIN, E. H. *Process Consultation: Its Role in Organization Development*. Menlo Park, Calif.: Addison-Wesley, 1969.

SCHEIN, E. H., AND BENNIS, W. G., *Personal and Organizational Change*

Through Group Methods: The Laboratory Approach. New York: Wiley, 1965.

SCHILDER, P. "Results and Problems of Group Psychotherapy in Severe Neurosis." *Mental Hygiene,* 1939, *23,* 87–98.

SCHUTZ, W. C. *Joy: Expanding Human Awareness.* New York: Grove Press, 1967.

SCHUTZ, W. C. *Here Comes Everybody.* New York: Harper and Row, 1971.

SEASHORE, C. "What is Sensitivity Training?" In R. T. Golembiewski and A. Blumberg (Eds.), *Sensitivity Training and the Laboratory Approach: Readings About Concepts and Application.* Itasca, Ill.: Peacock, 1970.

SECHREST, L. B., AND BARGER, B. "Verbal Participation and Perceived Benefit from Group Psychotherapy." *International Journal of Group Psychotherapy,* 1961, *11,* 49–59.

SHEPARD, H. A. "Explorations in Observant Participation." In L. P. Bradford, J. R. Gibb, and K. D. Benne (Eds.), *T-Group Theory and Laboratory Method: Innovation in Re-education.* New York: Wiley, 1964.

SHEPARD, H. A. "Changing Interpersonal and Intergroup Relationships in Organizations." In J. G. March (Ed.), *Handbook of Organizations.* Chicago: Rand-McNally, 1965.

SHEPARD, H. A. "Personal Growth Laboratories: Toward an Alternative Culture." *Journal of Applied Behavioral Science,* 1970, *6,* 259–266.

SHEPARD, M., AND LEE, M. *Marathon 16.* Richmond Hill, Ont.: Simon and Schuster of Canada, Ltd., 1971.

SIROKA, R. W., SIROKA, E. K., and SCHLOSS, G. A. *Sensitivity Training and Group Encounter.* New York: Grosset and Dunlap, 1971.

SLATER, P. *Microcosm: Structural, Psychological and Religious Evolution in Groups.* New York: Wiley, 1966.

SLATER, P. *The Pursuit of Loneliness.* Boston: Beacon Press, 1970.

SLAVSON, S. R. *An Introduction to Group Therapy.* New York: Commonwealth Fund, 1943.

SLAVSON, S. R. *A Textbook in Analytic Group Psychotherapy.* New York: International Universities Press, 1964.

SMITH, M. B. *Social Psychology and Human Values.* Chicago: Aldine, 1969.

SMITH, P. B. *T-Group Climate, Trainer Style and Some Tests of Learning.* Working paper. University of Sussex, 1967.

STOCK, D. "A Survey of Research on T-Groups." In L. P. Bradford, J. R. Gibb, and K. D. Benne (Eds.), *T-Group Theory and Laboratory Method: Innovation in Re-education*. New York: Wiley, 1964.

STOCK, D., and THELEN, H. A. *Emotional Dynamics and Group Culture*. New York: New York University Press, 1958.

STRUPP, H. H. "The Experiential Group and the Psychotherapeutic Enterprise." *International Journal of Group Psychotherapy*, 1973, *23* (2), 115–123.

TANNENBAUM, R., and DAVIS, S. "Values, Man and Organizations." In W. B. Eddy, W. W. Burke, V. A. Dupre, and O. South (Eds.), *Behavioral Science and the Manager's Role*. Washington, D.C.: NTL, 1969.

TIELHARD DE CHARDIN, P. *The Phenomenon of Man*. London: Collins, 1959.

TRIST, E. L., and SOFER, C. *Explorations in Group Relations*. Leicester, Eng.: Leicester University Press, 1959.

TRUAX, C. B. "The Process of Group Psychotherapy: Relationship Between Hypothesized Therapeutic Conditions and Interpersonal Exploration." *Psychological Monographs*, 1961, *75*, 1–35.

TUCKMAN, B. W. "Developmental Sequence in Small Groups." *Psychological Bulletin*, 1965, *63*, 384–399.

VONNEGUT, K. *Player Piano*. New York: Avon, 1970.

WENDER, L. "The Dynamics of Group Psychotherapy and Its Application." *Journal of Nervous and Mental Diseases*, 1936, *84*, 54–60.

WESCHLER, I., MASSARIK, F., and TANNENBAUM, R. "The Self in Process: A Sensitivity Training Emphasis." In I. Weschler and E. Schein (Eds.), *Issues in Human Relations Training Reading Series #5*. Washington, D.C.: NTL, 1962.

WESCHLER, I., AND SCHEIN, E. (Eds.) *Issues in Human Relations Training Reading Series #5*, Washington, D.C.: NTL, 1962.

WHITAKER, D. S., AND LIEBERMAN, M. A. "Assessing Interpersonal Behavior in Group Therapy." *Perceptual and Motor Skills*, 1964, *18*, 763.

WHITE, R. W. "Motivation Reconsidered: The Concept of Competence," *Psychological Review*, 1959, *66*, 293–333.

WHITMAN, R. "Psychodynamic Processes Underlying T-Group Processes." In L. P. Bradford, J. R. Gibb, and K. D. Benne (Eds.), *T-Group Theory and Laboratory Method: Innovation in Re-education*. New York: Wiley, 1964.

WINDER, A. E., AND HERSKO, M. "A Thematic Analysis of an Outpatient Psychotherapy Group." *International Journal of Group Psychotherapy*, 1958, *8*, 293–300.

WOLF, A. "The Psychoanalysis of Groups." *American Journal of Psychotherapy*, 1949, *3*, 16–50.

WOLF, A. "The Psychoanalysis of Groups." *American Journal of Psychotherapy*, 1950, *4*, 525–558.

YALOM, I. D. *The Theory and Practice of Group Psychotherapy*. New York: Basic Books, 1970.

YALOM, I. D., and RAND, K. "Compatibility and Cohesiveness in Therapy Groups." *Archives of General Psychiatry*, 1966, *13*, 267–276.

ঌঌঌঌঌঌঌ

Name Index

Subject Index

Ex Libris